THIS BOOK IS FOR:

_____

FROM:

_____

DATE:

_____

To Bob Ford

For your undying friendship,

And for the leaves of autumn.

A GOD NAMED

Desire

by

Ty Gibson

PACIFIC PRESS PUBLISHNG ASSOCIATION
Nampa, Idaho
Oshawa, Ontario, Canada

Design by GUILDHOUSE Group

ISBN 13: 978-0-8163-2397-5
ISBN 10: 0-8163-2397-6

Thank you . . .

Sue—first, foremost, and forever—because you keep on loving me into something more than I could ever be without you. And for making this book happen. Eternity baby!

Rachel Liem and Jenny Gruzensky for speed and accuracy, with smiles to boot.

Stephanie Van Koten-Hinger, Debra Meelhuysen, and Robert Erick for your eagle eyes.

Rosario brothers, because you're just totally cool and I love you.

Jasper Van Meurs for making me think and feel more deeply.

Jim Huenergardt for contagious creativity.

Fred Bischoff for teaching me so many rich perspectives.

James Rafferty for years and years of more than words can express.

The office study group for embracing this picture of God with such enthusiasm.

My Laurelwood class for motivating me. I really like you guys.

Dayna Turner for great photography at a moment's notice.

Jerry Thomas and all the good people at Pacific Press for seeing this vision over and over again.

Felix Mendelssohn and Ludwig Van Beethoven. A posthumous thank you makes no sense, so I'll just pay tribute by saying that most of this book was written in the stimulating audio atmosphere these men gave us. If there is anything like empirical proof of God's existence, the mathematical beauty of their musical genius is it.

PREFACE

This book is written for four kinds of people who are totally unlike one another in a lot of ways and totally like one another in one particular way to be divulged in the pages ahead.

1. Those who were raised with enough religion to make them feel obligated to God, but not attracted. Maybe God is more beautiful than you have ever imagined.

2. Those who feel skeptical about the existence of God, but not settled into unbelief. Maybe there are compelling ideas you've never considered.

3. Those who were raised with no religion at all and are not sure about God but are open to the phenomena of beauty, goodness, and love as holding some transcendent meaning you haven't yet figured out. Maybe all the attractive wonders of life to which you find yourself drawn point beyond themselves to a yet grander beauty, goodness, and love wooing you from afar.

4. Those who are believers in ideas about God, but are unbelievers in the person of God, and who find their faith in a passionless holding pattern lacking a vision of God that would ignite spontaneous adoration in their hearts. Maybe God isn't who you think He is.

To all these readers and any others who are hopeful for a more rational and attractive picture of God, welcome to something new . . . and really, really old! I invite you to the possibility of a dramatic shift on the landscape of reality by the simple introduction into your mind of a new idea—a new idea that traces all the way back to the self-giving Desire that first imagined you with extreme anticipation and eventually gave you existence. Whatever your response may be to what you are about to read, I am certain you will never see God or yourself the same again. Maybe this is the first day of the rest of your life, and it all gets exponentially better from here on.

CONTENTS

o n e

E N G I N E E R E D

Scientists are baffled by the mounting pile of evidence demonstrating that we humans are creatures engineered for love rather than mere biological survival machines as the theory of evolution dictates we should be.

But before we look at some current data, let's go all the way back to the thirteenth century when Frederick II, the German king and Holy Roman Emperor, conducted a cruel experiment intended to discover what language children would naturally grow up to speak if never spoken to.

He had a hunch it would be German. Some things just make sense, right?

Babies were taken from their parents at birth and placed in the care of nurses who were forbidden to speak in their hearing. An additional rule was imposed, as well, to prevent the nurses from bonding with the infants—no touch. All changing and feeding had to be conducted with utensils in order to ensure no physical contact. The diabolical study never yielded the information Frederick wanted, but it did reveal something far more significant regarding human nature. The babies grew up speaking no language at all—because they all died. In the year 1248, the Italian historian Salimbene recorded with an air of scientific observation, "They could not live without petting."

The newborns died for want of affectionate touch, which is to say they could not survive without the sense of love and connectedness that is communicated to the body and mind by touch. Modern medicine calls this phenomenon, "failure to thrive." For some reason we flourish under the influence of love, and we gradually die without it. Frederick's experiment revealed long ago what scientists are currently discovering to their absolute astonishment.

In his national best seller, *Love and Survival*, the famed Dr. Dean Ornish presents study after study to demonstrate that the human being is literally engineered for love. Ornish shows that love is the main factor involved in determining mental, emotional, and even physical health. Summarizing the "unexpected" message of the rapidly accumulating body of data, he says:

"Anything that promotes feelings of love and intimacy is healing; anything that promotes isolation, separation, loneliness, loss, hostility, anger, cynicism, depression, alienation, and related feelings often leads to suffering, disease, and premature death from all causes" (*Love and Survival*, p. 29).

Dr. Ornish is not using the word "love" as it is often defined in our pop culture. The data is indicating that human beings are psychologically and biologically dependent on *giving* love in the form of other-centered service, benevolence, affection and forgiveness, as well as on *receiving* love of the same character:

"What is also important in a number of studies is not only how much you *get* but also how much you *give*. Giving and receiving love and intimacy are healing for both the giver and for the recipient.

"In one study of more than seven hundred elderly adults, for example, the effects of aging had more to do with what they contributed to their social support network than what they received from it. The more love and support they offered, the more they benefited themselves" (Ibid., p. 29).

Ornish's research clearly indicates that we are wired for giving and receiving love, and that our health and survival depend on it. But this presents Dr. Ornish, and the entire scientific establishment, with an unsolved mystery. He states:

"The scientific evidence . . . leaves little doubt that love and intimacy are powerful determinants of our health and survival. *Why* they have such an impact remains somewhat a mystery" (Ibid., p. 22).

In an effort to resolve this mystery, Dr. Ornish interviewed a wide range of individuals who are experts in various fields of study, asking each one to address *why* human beings are so vitally dependent on love. The bottom-line answer that emerged was something like, "Well, it is odd, isn't it? We don't really know why."

After all his interviews with 22 highly educated specialists, Dr. Ornish concludes:

"Yet mystery remains. No one can fully explain what is going on, why love and intimacy matter so much" (Ibid., p. 171).

Trying to get to the bottom line of what his panel of experts had to say, Dr. Ornish says, "Many of these people talk about energy" (Ibid., p. 171).

Ah, yes, the ever elusive and featureless "energy." It's about the best explanation we can come up with short of acknowledging that reality has an ultimately personal explanation in an ultimately personal God. After all, it is understandable that the human dependency on love would be such a mystery for much of the scientific community. There are at least two reasons why:

First, modern science is trying to understand *love* within the framework of an *anti-love* model of reality. Beginning with a survival-of-the-fittest premise—which dictates that self-preservation must be the highest law and the main determinate of survival—love, which is essentially self-giving, makes no sense. Why would mere self-preserving evolutionary animals act in love toward others? Everyone knows that the evolutionary theory is mutually exclusive from any real altruistic impulse. If Darwinian natural selection is the truth of human origins, there is no such thing as love—plain and simple.

The second reason for the persisting mystery is connected with the first. Much of the scientific community insists on interpreting all empirical data with the presupposition that none of it could ever point to the existence of a personal supreme being. It is taken as a given that humans evolved from impersonal matter and, therefore, there is no personal dimension to ultimate reality. If the evolutionary theory were true, it would logically follow that we *should* be impersonal material creatures governed only by the instinct to survive. But here's where the problem arises: since much of the evidence strongly suggests that we are not mere biological survival machines, but rather that we are designed to operate optimally on the life-sustaining energy generated by love, this poses a serious break in the train of evolutionary logic. The existence of a personal God holds the kind of explanatory power we need to make sense of ourselves, but many scientists simply will not allow God to be figured into the picture of human origins. They are determined to find a reason for love without God being acknowledged. And the best they can do is to speak of a nebulous and impersonal "energy" that might be the source of this out-of-place phenomenon we call "love." Yet, it is clear that in the prevailing naturalistic model of reality, love should not exist. But it does and so we're baffled.

One of the scientists interviewed by Dr. Ornish states:

"I think that looking at this connection between relationship and survival is the most significant thing that can be done in our field right now. We are in a major crisis. We have tons of data with no theory, no way to connect all the little bits and pieces that have accumulated . . . no overriding conceptual model" (Ibid., p. 175).

In other words, we have tons of data all pointing to the unavoidable fact that we humans are somehow, for some reason, psychologically and biologically engineered for self-giving relationships, but we have no idea why we're like this, because if what we believe about the origin of life is true, we shouldn't be. And yet, the accumulating information points to something beyond any model of reality we have, or that we're willing to accept.

Jon Kabat-Zinn, Ph.D, another researcher interviewed by Dr. Ornish, affirmed that the findings of science are definitely indicating that human nature is innately designed for intimacy. So, logically, Dr. Ornish asked, "Intimacy with what?"

"Ultimately with the sense of self, with who you are," Kabat-Zinn answered. "Then, that 'I' itself becomes the object of awareness" (Ibid., p. 179).

He goes on to say that once we become intimate with ourselves as the highest reality to which we can relate, we come to realize that "the very notion of an 'I' is a delusion of consciousness. We've defined ourselves too narrowly" (Ibid., p. 179).

The empirical evidence of science is pointing beyond ourselves by telling us we are made for intimacy, but then the data is interpreted to mean that we must somehow need to achieve intimacy with ourselves, missing the point that intimacy with one's self is no intimacy at all, because intimacy is, by definition, connection with others.

Dr. Ornish himself can't see beyond the human self as the ultimate object of consciousness, and so he finds it necessary to define God in terms of a deified Self:

"God is not something we attain from 'out there' somewhere; we realize that God is *in* us *as* us... When understood in this context, the realization of God, of our Self by any other name, is perhaps the ultimate healing experience" (Ibid., p. 146).

The deepest rational sense of our hearts is speaking to us of the ultimate "Other," but we're trying hard not to listen. We're expecting the data to end up pointing to ourselves as the highest reality, except it's not pointing that way. What's happening on the frontiers of knowledge is that the more we know, the more obvious it's becoming that there is more to reality than the observable, material universe. But because science has pushed God out of the equation, we don't know what to do with data that point to Him. Within the very limited, confined parameters we have set for ourselves with the evolutionary model, we simply can't account for the phenomenon of love. In order to cope with the incongruent data, even the most hardcore empiricists, like Richard Dawkins, depart from science into conjecture by claiming that love is merely a sophisticated form of selfishness in disguise, a manifestation of evolution playing the survival-of-the-fittest game at a more highly evolved level. But that hypothesis is a desperate shot in the dark that denies the very existence of love, not to mention the fact that it leaves us cold and empty. The prevailing scientific assumption, which says we are merely evolving animals in a purely naturalistic universe void of any spiritual dimension, does not allow us to see the obvious—that we are beings in need of giving and receiving love because we were made in the image of a God whose essential nature is love.

At least Dr. Ornish recognizes that we are trying to understand our dependency on love within a scientific framework that simply does not allow for an answer:

"The current tools, models, and methods of inquiry of modern science are too limited to be able to answer fully the question of why love and intimacy have such powerful effects on health and healing. The question is not fully answerable from within the context of the inquiry. . . . If you are in the middle of a dream in which you are being chased by a tiger and you ask, 'How did I come to be chased by a tiger?' the question is not answerable from within the context of the dream. As long as you are dreaming, the dream seems very real, the tiger seems very dangerous and frightening. Only when you wake up do you realize the truth" (Ibid., p. 172).

Precisely!

Through science we have created a matrix of illusion for ourselves in
which our most basic assumptions about the nature of ultimate reality,
and about who and what we are, do not match up with life as we
actually experience it. From within the narrow parameters of our mental
confinement we can't explain to ourselves why we thrive on love and
wither without it. More puzzling still, we can't explain to ourselves why
we so desperately crave a quality of love that finds no match at all in
this world. Only when we "wake up" from the dream we've spun for
ourselves—this dark dream that places the human self at the pinnacle
of reality with nothing beyond us—only then will we "realize the truth."

Unavoidably, a tenacious desire for love haunts human
consciousness with what seems to be a wooing from afar. We try to
explain it with no reference point beyond ourselves, and we seek its
satisfaction in countless material pursuits.

But it remains,

larger than anything in this world can equal,

more persistent than our most determined resistance,

insistently fixed on something MORE than ourselves.

We can't help but ask the obvious question at some point:

What *is* that something more?

Has the desire that pulsates within us no suitable companion?

t w o

D E S I R E

y wife Sue thinks I'm a little weird for a guy. . . because I actually like shopping. She says I'm not supposed to. Girls like shopping, not guys. That's her take on it. But I'm a guy, and I like shopping. So I guess that blows her theory out of the water.

To make matters worse, even more un-guy-like, I guess, is the fact that my favorite place to shop is the grocery store. Not the tool store or the boat store or the car store, but the grocery store. Any grocery store will do.

Whenever Sue goes on the traditionally female expedition to get our food, I ask if I can go. She almost always says, "No!" in a rather emphatic tone. I think she hates the fact that I'm a better shopper than she is, me being a guy and all. I methodically go up and down every aisle, so I never forget anything, and I often discover new things to try, some of which have turned out to be quite yummy. She, on the other hand, shops like a man, like a hunter. She goes in and ricochets around like a pinball, nabbing only the items on her mental list. She's in and out of the store in a matter of minutes.

Boring.

Consequently, she often forgets things we need and never finds anything new. I think she knows in her heart that my method is better. But I don't press the issue. It's probably embarrassing for her as a woman that her husband is a better shopper than she is.

Anyway. . .

One day Sue assigned me the task of going to the store to secure the best salsa I could find for the Mexican dinner she was planning to make.

Sweet!

I love Mexican food.

"Please hurry," she pled. "Don't go up and down every aisle. Just get some salsa and get home."

So off to the store I went, determined to prove that I can, when necessary, shop like a man.

Upon entering the store, I went straight to the salsa aisle. But I encountered a problem that had the potential to slow me down a bit. There was a woman standing right in front of the salsa selection slowly examining the options.

"No big deal," I thought to myself. "I'll just wait my turn."

So, exercising proper grocery store etiquette, I politely came up behind her, standing slightly off to her left a foot or two back, casually looking over her shoulder at the options.

Suddenly, something strange and totally unexpected happened. Continuing her studied gaze forward at the salsa, she reached her left hand back and tenderly clasped mine in hers, and said, in a rather romantic tone,

"Medium or hot, sweetie pie?"

Needless to say, I was both nervous and flattered.

What was I to do? I was in a quandary. On the one hand, I knew I was not her sweetie pie. He must have been off in another aisle discovering new things. On the other hand, I do have very definite opinions about salsa, and she did ask my opinion. So there we stood holding hands. But I needed to hurry up and decide whether to release my hand from hers and divulge my true identity or to offer my salsa recommendation, because as she asked her question she was also slowly turning her head back toward mine, her lips in full pucker.

"Actually, ma'am," I said, craning my neck backwards toward the spaghetti sauce, "I prefer mild salsa. . ."

And just as I was about to explain that mild is best because it allows the eater to taste all the subtle fusion of the tomatoes, garlic, onions and cilantro, she yanked her hand from mine as if I had a contagious disease or something, sucked in her pucker, and made a mad dash out of the salsa aisle, no doubt searching for "sweetie pie."

Which was fine with me, because I needed to grab some salsa and hurry home.

I really did sympathize with the woman. It must have been truly freaky and frightening to turn her head expecting the familiar face of her true love, only to encounter a face she had never seen before. (Come to think of it, I sympathize more with me. It was not easy to offer my salsa advice under those circumstances.)

As I was rushing to the checkout stand to make my purchase, I was thinking two things.

First, I was hoping that sweetie pie was not 6'6" of tattoo-covered muscles searching the store for the salsa guy who had held his girl's hand.

Second, I was realizing anew that the human heart, every human heart, is also searching for its true love.

I know this to be a fact because there is something I know about you, although I've never met you. And it is the most personal and intimate thing of all. The reason I know this rather private info about you is because it's true of me as well, and of every other human being. It is the universal truism of human experience.

Even if you have never articulated this deeply personal thing to yourself, per se, as soon as I begin to name and explain it you will find yourself nodding in agreement, even if you are a little embarrassed to admit that it's true. But don't be shy about it, and don't feel nervous or threatened. Just allow yourself to contemplate the obvious.

Okay, I'll just blurt it out, although it may sound a little trite at first. But roll with me on it and see if it doesn't begin to resonate.

The thing you long for more than anything else is *To Love and Be Loved.*

Not in a silly, sentimental kind of way, but in a serious, substantial, life-defining sense. You want to experience a solid, deep, unalterable awareness that you are perfectly valued and cared for. You want to know with absolute certainty that there is someone you can trust with the full weight of your total reliance. You want to be completely confident that you are settled into an unfailing friendship that is grounded in honesty and integrity you can count on. You want to know that someone has given their life to you with unreserved commitment and loyalty.

And inextricably associated with the desire to receive love in the substantial way I've just described, is the tandem desire, perhaps even stronger, to be all of this to others.

You long to *be* a trustworthy friend,

to *be* loyal,

to *be* dependable,

to *be* devoted and forever true.

Even if you've corrupted your humanity and violated others (as we all have), you sometimes, on some level, wish you hadn't done those deeds and wish there was some way back to innocence.

To love and be loved!

Can you imagine anything better,

anything more meaningful,

anything more downright exhilarating?

Of course you can't.

Nothing else even comes close.

At the deepest level of your feeling heart, at the most rational level of your thinking mind, love is what you want and what you need. In your most sober, honest moments, you know that nothing less will suffice. And that's that. No ifs, ands, or buts about it.

Getting right to the core of the human psyche, the Bible makes this rather simple and insightful declaration:

"What a man desires is unfailing love" (Proverbs 19:22, NIV).

Here we have a general assessment about what's going on at the bedrock level of the human being. We somehow have this rather lofty and often seemingly fictitious idea about true love. We believe the real thing is actually out there somewhere to be had. So we keep hoping for it and looking for it. The notion shows up in nearly all the "once-upon-a-time" stories we tell ourselves. We want to be loved with a love that will never cease, never change, never come to an end.

The Bible calls it "unfailing love."

It's the absolute biggest and best idea conceivable.

And it's the only idea worthy of our humanity.

The first thing we need to understand about our insatiable desire for love is that it does not exist in a vacuum. We're like this for a reason. This latent longing for unfailing love pulsates in our hearts because we were originally made in the "image" of God, and "God *is* love" (Genesis 1:26; 1 John 4:8).

So it's an engineering issue.

Mentally, emotionally, and biologically we were engineered for love by a God whose essential character is love. We are what we are, and what we are is living love machines. Rational, sentient, volitional love machines. Except I don't really like the word *machine* in this setting, although it makes the point rather nicely, because what we're talking about here is what we are by design.

As we discovered in chapter one, we are wired for awareness of and sympathy for the others around us and for moving toward them in self-giving conduct. The inner workings of our mental and emotional faculties were created after the blueprint of the divine character. God is love, and we were made to think, feel, and live like God thinks, feels, and lives. Specific data was written into our DNA, into our very natures. The message and mandate encoded into the human system is, *Love and Be Loved!*

This is not about religion per se, as commonly defined. This is about getting to the core of identity—God's identity and the human identity, and the relation of the two. The Bible tells us who God is in character and who we are by His design. And then the Bible invites us to return to our true identity as creatures of the divine image—as receivers and dispensers of unfailing love.

Someone has observed:

"Creatures are not born with desires unless satisfaction for those desires exists. A baby feels hunger: well, there is such a thing as food. A duckling wants to swim: well, there is such a thing as water. Men feel sexual desire: well, there is such a thing as sex. If I find in myself a desire which no experience in this world can satisfy, the most probable explanation is that I was made for another world" (C.S. Lewis, *Mere Christianity*, p. 106).

All human wonderings and desires have some basis in reality. If God did not exist, we would not wonder if He does. And if God were anything less than perfect love, we would not long for such love. There would be a massive void in our consciousness where now there exists a massive desire for a love that transcends anything this world has to offer. As our Maker, God designed the inner workings of the human psyche in such a way that we have an innate sense, a divinely-implanted intuition, that we were made for eternal realities of a most fabulous and exhilarating nature. King Solomon observed, "He has put eternity in [our] hearts" (Ecclesiastes 3:11). We've been deliberately and supernaturally sculpted on the inside to yearn for eternal realities.

If you think long enough and hard enough, you can convince yourself that this lofty and magnificent view of reality isn't true. But you will be rationalizing against your very nature and against the most fundamental ideas that hang around in your head with a persistence that is at the very least suspicious, if not evidential. A little sober introspection tells us we are more than animals destined to fight for a transient survival, fulfill our physical urges for a few years, and then cease to exist.

All one need do is flip the evolutionary model and a startling perspective becomes conceivable: The human race is not engaged in an evolutionary process, but rather in a devolution process. We were not once something less and now have become something more. The opposite is the case: we were once something more and we have become something less. And yet, there are broken fragments of the divine image strewn around within us. The process of degeneration may be reversed if we will allow a healing hand to touch us deep on the inside of our wounded souls. We may return to the greatness for which we were made, to the lofty realm of love from which we've fallen.

It's as if we are afflicted with spiritual amnesia. We do not remember clearly who we are, but we get occasional flashes of recall, a sensing, a nameless knowing, that we came from a different place, a better situation, a reality of goodness, truth and beauty that we have somehow lost. We have an Edenic sense we can't shake. And the reason we can't shake it is because it's shaking us, stirring us, pulling us in. God is exerting a kind of gravitational pull on our souls:

"Yes, I have loved you with an everlasting love; therefore with lovingkindness I have drawn you" (Jeremiah 31:3).

He can't do otherwise.

Love *does* what love *is*.

God draws us with His love because, well, because He loves us. That's all, and that's enough. That's all the reason love needs. He simply longs for us and therefore He is drawing us. God's heart is a massive vortex of unstoppable love constantly pulling us in. He pulls us toward Himself with an eternal quality of love, a love that cannot cease to love anymore than God can cease to exist. The power of the pull lies in the fact that God's love is gorgeously attractive with substance and meaning and moral integrity. It tells us who and what we are by creation and what we ought to be by redemption and by choice. When we get glimpses of it—sometimes from the corner of our eye, sometimes in a full-frontal realization— we are drawn.

Powerfully drawn.

The Hebrew prophets understood that one day God would materialize His love in a living person who would perfectly answer to the universal human longing. The prophet Haggai ascribed an extremely insightful title to this coming One:

"The Desire of All Nations" (Haggai 2:7).

The Craving of All Hearts.

The Universal Yearning.

When this Desirable One landed in our world, He said things like:

I am the bread of life. Eat Me and you will never be hungry again (John 6:35-58).

I am the water of life. Drink Me and you will never thirst again (John 4).

I am your friend. Live in My love and your joy will be full (John 15:10-15).

Jesus was, and is, the embodiment of the unfailing love for which we were made, and for which we yearn.

"I, when I am lifted up," He boldly declared, "will draw all peoples to Myself" (John 12:32, AB).

Big claim, I know, but not an exaggeration if we understand what He's saying. In the overall context, Jesus explained that He would voluntarily lay down His own life out of sheer love for every human being (John 12:23-28; 15:13; 10:15, 18). So when Jesus said He would draw *all* hearts to Himself, what He meant, essentially, was that He would demonstrate in His life and death the quality of love that every heart needs and desires. And that demonstration of divine love is so powerful that when we see it for what is really means, a sympathetic resonance will awaken within us. What we behold in *that* singular manifestation of self-giving love will ring true to what God has been whispering into our hearts all along. It will correspond to the everlasting love with which God has been drawing our hearts since our first moments of consciousness.

We see Him freely forgiving the shame-laden woman, and something inside us says, *Yes, that's what God ought to be like and that's what I need!*

We see Him calling the oppressive, hypocritical religious leaders to account, and liberating the people from their narrow, clenched-fist portrayal of God, and we say, *Yes, that's what I would expect from God—justice for the oppressed!*

We see Him touching the outcasts, healing the sick, feeding the hungry, relieving the sorrowing, and we say, *Yes, that's a God worthy of worship!*

Finally, we see Him receiving all the violence hateful men could heap upon Him while freely forgiving them. We watch as He lays down His life because He loves each of us more than His own existence, and we say, *Wow, now that's real love, and that's what I desire and need more than anything else!*

This is the One we've been waiting for.

The One we all desire.

He is *the* Desire

of *all* nations

and of *every* heart.

And, as we will now discover, the only reason we desire Him is because He desires us.

three

M U S I C

A little boy sat on the piano bench clumsily poking at the keys, pretending to read the open piece of sheet music. Deeply moved by the precious sight, Daddy sat beside him.

"When you were in Mommy's tummy," he said to the boy, "I would often have her sit right here with me and I would play this very song to you."

To the father's utter surprise, the boy casually replied, "Oh, so that was *you!*"

Whether the little guy actually recalled hearing the father's music or not, we do know that babies in the womb do hear many sounds from just the other side of the mother's thin belly wall.

Do you?

Hear the Father's music, that is?

According to the prophet Zephaniah, God does, in fact, sing over you, and over me as well:

"The Lord your God is with you, He is mighty to save. He will take great delight in you, He will quiet you with His love, He will rejoice over you with singing" (Zephaniah 3:17, NIV).

This is the Bible's poetic way of telling us that God is very aware of us, very sensitive toward us, and that He is trying to get ideas about His love for us into our heads. So God sings. From just the other side of the thin wall that separates the seen from the unseen, He serenades our hearts, constantly whispering the truth of His love into our consciousness. There is some real but inaudible sense in which God's thoughts and feelings, like a song, are floating sweetly into our hearts. And as He sings over us, He is hoping we will hear His song and come to know His heart.

The very idea that God sings at all is actually quite an astounding revelation about the kind of being this Almighty Creator must be.

What kind of person sings anyway?

Well, first of all, a very personal kind of person, a person with thoughts they want to express and feelings they want others to feel.

That's the sort of God we're dealing with here.

Not the "Unmoved Mover" kind of God Aristotle would have us imagine.

Not the "impassible" and "deterministic" God of Classical Theism, which is merely a Christianized version of Aristotle's God.

Not the "impersonal force" or the "collective soul" of Pantheism and Star Wars ("May the Force be with you!").

None of these match up with the character profile of the God revealed in Scripture.

A God who sings must be a God who feels, a God of deep, stirring passions. If God sings, and the Bible says He does, then we find ourselves living in the presence of a Supreme Being whose heart pulsates with supreme emotion.

The implications are huge.

Some ancient Greek hippies called the Pythagoreans observed that all of creation is mathematical, which you have no doubt noticed as well. Then they noticed that music is math, as well. They realized that music is mathematically composed in such a manner that it creates new thoughts and feelings in the human soul. So they came up with a hypothesis: the Creator must be a singer and He must have sung the universe into existence; the entire cosmos must operate on a musical score of some kind.

Who knows, maybe the Pythagoreans were right. Music is emotional math, after all, and the lyrics that attend music are simply emotionally rendered thoughts. The great composers believed they were giving musical voice to the beauties of creation through their art. Some of them claimed that music occurred to their imaginations as they observed the wonders of the world around them, as if they were hearing something that was already there. They thought they were engaged more in a process of discovering music than in a process of creating it.

The God of the Bible is the omnipotent Creator of all things. The sheer magnitude and gravity of the idea that there is such a being can be rather overwhelming and intimidating. Even terrifying.

But if God sings . . . well, that changes everything.

It opens our minds to the realization that within all this enormous power there beats a tender heart.

If God sings, we find ourselves standing in awe before the union of absolute might housed within infinite sensitivity.

And it means even more.

Because if God is a composer and singer of love songs, as Scripture says He is, that means He must be deeply in love with us, because only those who are in love sing love songs. And it must also mean He wants us to hear Him, because singers who sing love songs sing to be heard by the ones they love.

The question is, do we?

Do we hear the divine music?

I'll never forget my own, "Oh-so-that-was-you" awakening.

I was eighteen years old. To that point I had never been exposed to the idea of God, had never read a single piece of religious literature. I knew absolutely nothing about God, and very little about religion. And yet there were things I somehow did know, and some of those things I knew with intense conviction and strong emotions. I was filled with a palpable rage at the injustice and oppression in our world. I knew men shouldn't abduct children and brutalize them. I knew women should not be beaten by their husbands. I knew nations shouldn't drop bombs on one another, that people shouldn't starve to death while others eat more than health requires, that drug dealers shouldn't prey on kids, and that people should not hate others because they have a different skin color.

And I knew something more, something even more fundamental.

I knew the fact that I knew certain things to be bad meant there had to be some actual and ultimate good that defined the bad by contrast. And I'd get glimpses of the good sometimes,

like when I'd see a man love his child,

or two children laughing their heads off enjoying one another's friendship, or a person intervene with courage to stop an injustice,

or when I'd encounter the beauty of nature,

or even in the longing for love expressed in a song.

I knew all these things without knowing God. But as I realized later, I knew these things because He knew me. He had been singing to my soul all along, but I didn't know it was Him.

Then the day came when my rage against evil and my desire for good to prevail found resonance in an encounter with the One who is the source of the good and the enemy of the bad. It was like putting a face with a name, or actually more like putting a name with a face. In my heart I had a strong sense of what the world might be like if no injustice was ever committed, if nobody ever violated anyone else, if everyone cared more about others than for themselves. When I realized that the Creator of our world was the matrix of the good I longed for, and that He hated all the evil and injury, I was like the little boy at the piano with his dad:

"Oh, so that was you!"

It dawned on me that if I were merely an evolving animal, then no higher aspiration than survival would present itself to me. In a flash of imparted insight I suddenly understood that I only hated evil because there is such a thing as evil, and that I only longed for goodness because there is such a thing as an ultimate good. And now I had located the absolute antithesis of evil and the absolute epicenter of goodness—in a personal God who had created humanity in His image. It was this God who, all my life, was interjecting a steady stream of moral stimuli into my conscience, guiding and prompting me. Now I knew the name of the One who had been singing over my soul.

It was like the time I was driving down the road and I heard this amazing song on the radio. I felt I must hear it again. Grabbing a pen and a scrap of paper, I prepared to write the information down.

But to my utter frustration, the DJ just went on his merry way playing the next song and never identified the source of the masterpiece that had captured my attention.

A couple years passed by. Then one day a friend of mine asked if I had ever heard Samuel Barber's *Adagio*. I told him I had not. "You must hear it," he insisted. A few days later he gave me the CD as a gift, urging me to sit down immediately and listen to it with him.

As soon as the beautiful strings began to rise like morning sunlight breaking through the cold winter fog, I knew this was the song.

"Yes, I know this song," I told my friend. "I heard it once a couple of years ago and it's been playing in my head ever since."

The source of the song in my head was finally found.

Have you made the connection between the song of love that persists in your heart and its divine Composer?

four

K N O C K I N G

*G*he idea of intentional divine communication to all human beings is pervasive throughout Scripture. Not only is God singing to us, there is also some sense in which He's knocking.

If "God is love," as the Bible says He is, then we'd expect Him to knock before entering. That's how love operates. It honors individual freedom. We have a very ugly word for forced love. We call it "rape." And we know it's not love at all, but rather a gross distortion. The God who courts our affections in the person of Christ is in possession of unfathomable power, and yet He chooses to hold that power in reserve in favor of knocking, which means, in favor of our freedom.

"Behold, I stand at the door and knock. If anyone hears My voice and opens the door, I will come in to him and dine with him, and he with Me" (Revelation 3:20).

Could almighty power take on any more attractive form? The only person in the universe who actually could force us into subjection and be answerable to nobody above Himself, simply chooses not to.

And why?

Only one answer presents itself: because His ultimate objective is bilateral love, not unilateral control. Which, oddly enough, or not so oddly, is the only kind of God we might actually want to give control of our lives. Make no mistake about it, God does most definitely want in. But He only wants in by invitation, because He only wants in for purposes of mutual engagement. The beauty of this idea, this truth, this picture of God, is so attractive that it will pull us into Him if we start to believe it.

The word "behold" in our passage means, *Take notice. Understand. Get this.*

The word "knock" indicates an effort to get our attention. It's the divine, *Hey! Excuse Me! May I have your attention please!* And the fact that He calls the knocking, "My voice," suggests that God is on a communication quest, speaking intelligible truths into our awareness.

The plea to "open" presupposes the reality of freewill and the metaphysical fact that the human heart can only be unlatched from the inside.

Unlatched?

Yes.

There are mental and emotional locks we have set up inside ourselves to avoid getting hurt. There are defenses erected within our souls. There are even survival lies we tell ourselves so we don't have to become vulnerable to God's overtures. And the only way for God to get us to unlatch the door to our hearts and let Him in is by communicating the reassuring truth of His love and goodwill. That's the knocking, and it's been happening all your life in multiple ways. It's happening even now as you read this book and encounter new ideas that seem strangely attractive and even familiar.

God's invitation to "dine with" Him communicates the idea of fellowship. He wants a rich interpersonal relationship with you, a connection that involves the exchange of thoughts and feelings.

God is basically saying, "Take notice of the fact that I am standing right outside the door of your heart, of your consciousness, trying to get your attention with love and not with force. If you hear My knocking, all you have to do is open your heart by an act of freewill, and I will come in to you. I'll come into your thinking and feeling process, and we will begin a relationship with one another. I will feed your heart and mind with information, insights, and truths that will nourish and strengthen our relationship. And you will bless Me, as well, with your returning love."

On whose heart does the gentlemanly divine knocking persist?

To whom exactly is this "voice" speaking, and what does it say?

Moses gave the Israelites the Ten Commandments that God had written on sapphire stone. He then expounded the Law by giving them numerous additional instructions that made application of the Ten Commandments to every aspect of daily life. Then he looped back to distill all these laws down to a single law:

". . .to love the Lord your God with all your heart and with all your soul, that you may live" (Deuteronomy 30:6).

That's the law of God.

Love.

Other-centeredness.

Pure, simple, and profoundly meaningful.

Moses then threw the Israelites, and us, a curve ball of insight:

"This commandment which I command you today, it is not too mysterious for you, nor is it far off. It is not in heaven, that you should say, 'Who will ascend into heaven for us and bring it to us, that we may hear it and do it?' Nor is it beyond the sea, that you should say, 'Who will go over the sea for us and bring it to us, that we may hear it and do it?' But the word is very near you, in your mouth and in your heart, that you may do it" (Deuteronomy 30:11-12, 14).

Moses says, in essence, "The truth I've been explaining to you is self-evident and obvious. In fact, you already know it if you'd just stop and think it through, if you'd just be honest. I'm not telling you anything new or mysterious or far out. It's not way up in heaven, nor is it off in some foreign land over the ocean. It's so close, in fact, that it's on your lips in the things you say, and it's in your own heart in the way you think and feel. The law of love is inscribed in your very nature, although you are living in violation of it."

Every time a human being speaks of right and wrong, fairness and justice, or of any moral parameters at all, the mouth belies all our claimed ignorance and unbelief. As his concluding argument, a theist said to an atheist, "I am glad to hear that you don't believe in God or any transcendent standard of moral right or wrong, because I'll be leaving tonight with your wallet, your car, and your wife." Immediately the atheist was a believer in something, against his rational arguments, of course, but in accordance with an impulsive rationale that kicked into high gear the moment he was faced with the idea of a moral violation.

We know more than we'd like to admit at times. Every time a human heart feels a sense of disapproval for doing wrong or a sense of affirmation for doing good, the essence of the encompassing truth of God's love is known in the soul. In our moments of heightened moral sense we are brought face to face with the truth that has been speaking to our hearts all along.

"What may be known of God is manifest *in them*, for God has shown it to them" (Romans 1:19).

In them?

Yes, in them, in their very nature as creatures of the divine image.

He's singing.

He's knocking.

He's speaking.

God is engaged in a universal revelation project, and every human heart is at the receiving end. Paul goes on to explain in Romans 2 that the principles of God's law are self-evident to human hearts even if we don't have the law before us as a written moral code:

"When Gentiles, who do not have the law, by nature do the things in the law, these, although not having the law, are a law to themselves, who show the work of the law written in their hearts, their conscience also bearing witness, and between themselves their thoughts accusing or else excusing them" (Romans 2:14-15).

These are remarkable and elementary insights, and more remarkable than elementary. In so many words, Paul is telling us that the truth is inescapable because it is innate to the way we are made. The law of God is not an arbitrary set of rules foreign to our minds unless it be told to us and imposed on us. Rather, God's law is intrinsic to all of reality as God made reality to function, including human nature.

So even if a person grows up in a culture that never affords him or her an encounter with God's law as a written code, that person will still know that certain actions constitute violations of others and certain actions constitute right ways of relating to others. When we do wrong, our conscience accuses us. When we do right, it affirms us.

Plain and simple—*we know.*

We may lie to ourselves, but *we know.*

We may rationalize our selfish deeds, but *we know.*

We may excuse our failure to treat people with respect, deference and love, but *we know.*

We may philosophize God out of existence, but *we know.*

And what, specifically, do we know?

Heaps, actually.

We know love, for "God is love," and He's the One speaking to us as the Revealer of what we know. We deny it and we violate it, but we know love.

We know that there is a *me* and there is a *you*, that we are distinct persons, that there is a neutral space between us, that there is a neutral material world in that space between us, and that we can cross that neutral space and utilize that neutral material to love one another or violate one another. We know love, because we know that the right relationship of self to all others is one of self-giving benevolence.

We know what love is in theory and what it ought to be in practice.

We know that love means doing what is good and right and true toward all others.

We know that to have the advantage is a grave responsibility and that no other person should be injured by our advantage, and, in fact, that those who are disadvantaged should be helped by us due to our advantage.

We know that being rude to the slow lady at the grocery store is wrong.

We know that children should never be abused.

That hungry people should be fed.

That oppressed people should be liberated.

That getting richer and richer and turning a blind eye to the needy while buying more and more stuff for ourselves is greed.

We know that marriage vows are to be kept.

That control and manipulation are dehumanizing.

That the frail, the weak, and the elderly should be properly cared for.

We even know that we shouldn't cut in line, cut off the car in front of us, or keep the extra $20 the cashier accidentally gave us.

But we know more than right from wrong and innocence from guilt. We know that right and wrong, that innocence and guilt, are essentially relational in nature. So we know, if we're honest, that we were made for the ultimate relationship with the ultimate Person.

We know that Someone of enormous and beautiful personhood is trying to get our attention.

We know that in all the promptings of our conscience, in all our recoiling at injustice, in all our longings for goodness to somehow, someday, win, that we are hearing the singing, the knocking, and the speaking of the Maker of our souls.

five

CONCENTRIC

The prophet Ezekiel rather abruptly opens his book with the startling claim, "I saw visions of God" (Ezekiel 1:1).

Astounded and extremely curious we might ask, "Visions of God, Ezekiel, God Himself?"

"Yes," he would reply, "God."

"Well then, do tell us, what exactly did you see when you saw God?"

The prophet's description is truly amazing.

"Then I looked, and behold, a whirlwind was coming out of the north, a great cloud with raging fire engulfing itself, and brightness was all around it and radiating out of its midst like the color of amber, out of the midst of the fire" (Ezekiel 1:4).

Here Ezekiel offers us some extremely illuminating insight regarding who and what manner of personage God is. I saw God, he reports, and what I saw looked like a "whirlwind" of "raging fire engulfing itself" and "radiating" outward.

The old King James Version says, "a fire enfolding itself."

Another translation renders the Hebrew text, "flames of fire coming after one another" (Bas).

What is fire but the expenditure of energy? And yet, all forms of energy with which we are familiar burn down and out to a cold end. But not this fire. This fire is an ever-replenishing expenditure. It never weakens. Never ceases. Never grows cold. Because this fire is eternal God engaged in some kind of infinitely sustained action.

We are called upon by Ezekiel to envision a raging fire burning in circular motion.

Huh!

An enfolding kind of movement is depicted, flame following flame in a rotational motion of perpetual energy. Interaction is occurring within this sublime reality called God. Association of a fervent sort is happening. Divinity is alive and moving, extending out and receiving in, one flaming entity reaching out "after" another, each one "enfolding" the other in massive bursts of fiery energy.

God On Fire

Throughout the Bible, as one of its most prominent features, God is associated with fire.

Moses encountered God "in a flame of fire from the midst of a bush. So he looked and behold, the bush was burning with fire, but the bush was not consumed" (Exodus 3:2).

The Ten Commandment Law of God is called a "fiery law" (Deuteronomy 33:2-3).

Assessing Israel's encounter with God, Moses said, "The sight of the glory of the Lord was like a consuming fire on the top of the mountain in the eyes of the children of Israel" (Exodus 24:17).

In Solomon's epic love song, the passion that flows so beautifully between the lover and his beloved is depicted as "flames of fire, the very flame of the LORD." And this flaming love is said to be so strong that it is unquenchable (Song of Solomon 8:6-7, NASB).

The prophet Daniel says that God's "throne" is "a fiery flame, its wheels a burning fire; a fiery stream issued and came forth from before him" (Daniel 7:9-10).

And the apostle Paul states succinctly, "Our God is a consuming fire" (Hebrews 12:29).

So then, God's *presence* is described as fire. God's *law* is said to be fiery in some sense. God's *glory* was seen by the Israelites as fire. God's *love* is depicted as an unquenchable fire. God's *throne* is a fiery flame with some kind of burning wheels extending from it. And a river of fire flows forth from God. Everything about God is ablaze with outgoing, radiating energy of some sort.

But what does all this fiery language mean?

Of course God is not literally composed of fire or mere energy. God is not an impersonal element or force. The divine nature is beyond our finite comprehension, so we can't even begin to define it. But God's *character* is comprehensible, and Ezekiel's vision points in that direction.

The laws of logic dictate that if A=B and B=C, then it is also true that A=C. If God's law=fire, and God's glory=fire, and God's love=fire, and God's throne=fire, then there is some sense in which God's law, God's glory, God's love, and God's throne are all precisely the same reality. In other words, the core truth about God may be described in terms of law, or glory, or love, or throne, but in each instance

Scripture is talking about the same basic principle of action that defines God's essential identity.

Putting the pieces together, the picture that emerges is truly breathtaking.

Wonder of wonders, at the center of reality, where life unborrowed and original resides in its uniquely immortal divine form, there exists nothing less than the most beautiful thing imaginable:

total self-giving passion, ever burning but never ceasing;

a fire of pure life enfolding itself while simultaneously reaching outward;

a radiant glory of plural personhood engaged in an eternal cycle of giving, serving, and caring;

an extravagant lavishing of love one upon another.

To know God in this light is to know God as God is and to know the meaning of life in the most elementary and profound sense.

Ezekiel brings to our awareness the fundamental truth of God's identity by revealing that God lives in perpetual other-centered motion, engaged eternally in an ever-replenishing outpouring of love, a raging hot passion that never ceases and never weakens. It burns and burns and burns, but never diminishes. God is sheer life acting always in the best interest of others—constant, thriving, undying. God is love, and as such, God is pure desire focused completely outward.

But now, let's ask the question that logically arises in the light of such a magnificent reality: what are the implications for all created life that exists residual to the life of love that pulsates at the matrix of the universe? And more specifically, what are the implications for you and me as individual persons living in a universe created by this kind of God?

I invite you to watch now as the picture enlarges, circling out from the raging fire at the center of reality until our own place in the beautiful vision becomes clear.

Prophets See Things For Us

Prophets are seers. They see things we humans don't ordinarily see. Their eyes are allowed to penetrate into spiritual mysteries. And their vision allows us access to information we need in order to construct an accurate sense of who God is and who we are in relation to Him.

If we correlate Ezekiel's vision with additional visions of the heavenly realm received by Moses, Daniel, and John, an enlightening picture of God's character and kingdom emerges. We come to understand that God's governmental structure is composed of a series of concentric circles. If you stop and think about it, this is the very shape we would expect to encounter if God is love, because love is, by its very nature, concentric. If love were to be represented geometrically, its shape could only be depicted as a circle. And if love were to be represented operationally, the circle would need to be moving. Love is round and rotational. Individual selves engage in love-like motion only insofar as they pour out of themselves into others.

It is a note-worthy fact that reality at all levels is basically round in shape and circular in motion. Think of the planetary systems and how they move. Think of the ecosystem. Think of biology and the circulatory system. Think of sociology, psychology and economics, even of computer science. All we see everywhere we look is one intersecting wheel within another. Everything appears to be geared toward giving and receiving, and everything that ceases to give and receive tends to wane and die. It should come as no surprise, then, that the picture of God's character and kingdom given to us by the prophets is a beautifully concentric one.

The Two Covering Cherubim

Our picture begins with the central fixture we've already put in place—the raging fire enfolding itself and radiating outward, which is Ezekiel's description of God engaged in perpetual love.

Next we turn to Moses for insight. As one of God's closest confidants, Moses was called by the Lord up onto a mountain to receive precise architectural specifications for building a tabernacle as a miniature likeness of heavenly realities.

"Let them make Me a sanctuary," God said to Moses, "that I may dwell among them. According to all that I show you, that is, the pattern of the tabernacle and the pattern of all its furnishings, just so you shall make it" (Exodus 25:8-9).

Paul explained that the pattern Moses received was a "copy and shadow of the heavenly things" (Hebrews 8:5). The sanctuary was a simple symbolic model of things in the heavenly realm.

At the center of the sanctuary was an inner room in the shape of a cube. It was called the Most Holy Place or the Holy of Holies. Within this room was one article of furniture called the Ark of the Covenant. It was so named because it contained the tablets of stone engraved with the Ten Commandments, also known as "the Covenant" (Exodus 34:28). Upon the ark was a solid gold lid called "the mercy seat" (Exodus 25:17). On either end of the mercy seat were two gold angelic figures called the "two cherubim" (Exodus 25:18-19). Moses was instructed that "the cherubim shall stretch out their wings above, covering the mercy seat with their wings, and they shall face one another; the faces of the cherubim shall be toward the mercy seat" (Exodus 25:20). Then God told Moses, "And there I will meet with you, and I will speak with you from above the mercy seat, from between the two cherubim which are on the ark" (Exodus 25:22). Indicating that the cherubim are positioned in God's immediate presence, a biblical songwriter sings, "You who dwell between the cherubim, shine forth!" (Psalm 80:1).

Additional insight from Ezekiel informs us that Lucifer, the fallen angel who is now called Satan, was one of these two covering cherubs before his rebellion. The prophet heard God address Lucifer: "You were the anointed cherub who covers; I established you" (Ezekiel 28:14). The position vacated by Lucifer was obviously filled by another angel since the Bible continues to indicate that there are still two covering cherubim. It is highly likely that the angel named Gabriel is one of the current two cherubim, either Lucifer's replacement or one of the original two. He appeared to Zacharias, the father of John the Baptist, and stated his position in the divine government: "I am Gabriel, who stands in the presence of God, and was sent to speak to you" (Luke 1:19).

We conclude, then, that the two covering cherubim are beings whose specific station or office of responsibility has them positioned in the immediate presence of God. Father, Son, and Holy Spirit compose the primary circle of fellowship at the center of the universe, while this high-ranking angelic duo occupies the second circle out from the divine inner circle.

The Four Living Creatures

Turning our attention to the apostle John, we discover that there are "four living creatures" that compose the third circle in the heavenly structure.

Introducing his vision of the heavenly realm, John says, "I looked, and behold, a door standing open in heaven. . . . Immediately I was in the Spirit; and behold, a throne set in heaven, and One sat on the throne" (Revelation 4:1-2). The one seated on the throne is God the Father. Later in the vision John tells us that Christ is with the Father "in the midst of the throne" and that the Holy Spirit is also present (Revelation 5:6-7). Then John describes the four living creatures:

"Before the throne there was a sea of glass, like crystal. And in the midst of the throne, and around the throne, were four living creatures full of eyes in front and in back" (Revelation 4:6).

Who are these extraordinary beings and what role do they play in the divine government?

Ezekiel offers us additional insight. Like John after him, Ezekiel saw the four living creatures around the throne of God. John merely described them. Ezekiel explained what they actually do. After giving us his description of God as a "raging fire enfolding itself," Ezekiel says, "from within it came the likeness of four living creatures" (Ezekiel 1:4-6). He goes on for a few verses to give additional details regarding the physical appearance of the creatures. Then he launches into a fascinating description of the manner in which they operate.

The first thing we notice about the office occupied by these living creatures is that they are a unit of four equally ranking beings. This is evident from the fact that they are described as identical in appearance, as performing the same duties, and as forming a circle, or one translation says a "square," around God's throne with their "wing tips touching" (Ezekiel 1:9, TEV).

As a unit of equals, the four creatures receive a continual stream of communication from a particular fiery entity. Ezekiel says, "Among the creatures there was something that looked like a blazing torch, constantly moving. The fire would blaze up and shoot out flashes of lightning. The creatures themselves darted back and forth with the speed of lightning" (Ezekiel 1:13-14, TEV).

If we correlate John's throne-room vision with what Ezekiel saw, it seems that the fiery entity that rushes back and forth among the four living creatures is the Holy Spirit. John states:

"From the throne proceeded lightning, thunderings, and voices. Seven lamps of fire were burning before the throne, which are the seven Spirits of God. Before the throne there was a sea of glass, like crystal. And in the midst of the throne, and around the throne, were four living creatures full of eyes in front and in back" (Revelation 4:5-6).

The Holy Spirit is pluralized here with the number seven to symbolize the Spirit's utter perfection, not to suggest that there are literally seven Holy Spirits. Later John speaks of "seven horns and seven eyes, which are the seven Spirits of God sent out into all the earth" (Revelation 5:6). In Scripture, horns are a symbol of power and eyes are a symbol of discernment or wisdom. Since the number seven indicates perfection, we gather from John's vision that the Holy Spirit possesses perfect power and perfect wisdom. Remarkably, John says that all this power and wisdom is being applied to the inhabitants of earth, which takes us back to Ezekiel's vision.

As the Holy Spirit assigns missions to the four living creatures, they are also seen to be moving back and forth among their own ranks:

"The living creatures ran [sped, NIV] back and forth, in appearance like a flash of lightning. Now as I looked at the living creatures, behold, a wheel was on the earth beside each living creature with its four faces. The appearance of the wheels and their workings was like the color of beryl, and all four had the same likeness. The appearance of their workings was, as it were, a wheel in the middle of a wheel. When they moved, they went toward any one of the four directions; they did not turn aside when they went" (Ezekiel 1:14-17).

Obviously we are being shown something elaborate, large, and highly organized. The language indicates a perpetual stream of activity surrounding and issuing from the throne room. But what exactly is the system of wheels composed of? Ezekiel gives additional details:

"As for their rims, they were so high [enormous] they were awesome; and their rims were full of eyes, all around the four of them. When the living creatures went, the wheels went beside them; and when the living creatures were lifted up from the earth, the wheels were lifted up. Wherever the spirit wanted to go, they went, because there the spirit went; and the wheels were lifted together with them, for the spirit of the living creatures was in the wheels [or, "the wheels did exactly what the creatures did, because the creatures controlled them" (TEV)]" (Ezekiel 1:18-20).

Now the picture becomes a bit clearer.

Wheels indicate rotational motion. These wheels are moving from heaven to earth and back again. Eyes indicate intelligence. There are always faces behind eyes. The wheels are full of eyes because the wheels are composed of large numbers of angels under the command of the living creatures. The fact that each of the systems extending from each of the four creatures is composed of a wheel within a wheel indicates that each retinue of angels is itself engaged in additional levels of organization. Ezekiel is describing for us a colossal network of angelic activity under the generalship of the four living creatures, all focused on planet Earth. Each of the creatures with their highly organized wheels of angels, millions upon millions of them, are engaged in a moment-by-moment execution of assignments on behalf of men, woman, and children in need.

This interpretation harmonizes with the picture communicated throughout Scripture of the angels and their work. According to the Bible, the angelic order is, in fact, involved in a non-stop stream of travel to our little world to perform intervening missions of mercy. Jesus told His disciples that He constitutes in some sense a ladder upon which the angels ascend and descend between heaven and earth (John 1:51). Jesus also stated that children are attended by angels who look continually upon the face of God on behalf of the little ones (Matthew 18:10). Paul explained that literally "all" of the angels are constantly being "sent forth to minister for those who will inherit salvation"—not *some* or even *most*, but "all" (Hebrews 1:14). He went so far as to caution us, "Do not forget to entertain strangers; for by so doing some have unwittingly entertained angels" (Hebrews 13:2).

The Angelic Armies
As we briefly noticed earlier, the prophet Daniel received a vision of God upon this throne. In that vision he also saw a massive army of angels around the Lord.

"The Ancient of Days was seated; His garment was white as snow, and the hair of His head was like pure wool. His throne was a fiery flame, its wheels a burning fire; a fiery stream issued and came forth from before Him. A thousand thousands ministered to Him; ten thousand times ten thousand stood before Him" (Daniel 7:9-10).

Like Ezekiel, Daniel sees God enveloped in fire. His throne is ablaze. A river of fire flows from Him. Like Ezekiel, Daniel also sees wheels of activity extending from God's throne. But Daniel adds another specific feature of the heavenly organizational structure. While Daniel does not mention the two covering cherubim or the four living creatures, he does offer us a view of the angelic armies that serve the kingdom.

Daniel sees two circles of angelic forces. First he mentions "a thousand thousands," which is one million. These, he says, "minister" to the One on the throne. As an elite inner circle of angels, perhaps this regiment of one million strong fulfills special missions directly commanded by the Lord since they are said to specifically "minister" to Him. Then Daniel says he saw a much larger group: "ten thousand times ten thousand stood before Him," which would be one hundred million. This is likely the massive army that composes the living wheels full of eyes that Ezekiel saw extending to earth under the charge of the four creatures.

Whether or not Daniel has given us precise numbers isn't the point. What we do clearly see is that God is surrounded by an elaborate system of workers. They fill positions of responsibility and stand ready to execute whatever assignments they might be given. Correlating the visions of Daniel and Ezekiel, an organizational system becomes evident. The Father, the Son, and the Holy Spirit compose the epicenter of all love, service, and power. Beside them are the two covering cherubim, the highest-ranking individuals in the kingdom. Next are the four living creatures that lead the angelic armies, and the angelic armies are composed of at least "a thousand thousands" and "ten thousand times ten thousand."

But there's still more to the picture.

The Twenty-four Elders
As we followed through in describing the four living creatures and the angel-armies they command, we skipped over another group of individuals that circle the presence of God.

Positioned at some station around the throne—it would seem in between the four living creatures and the two circles of the angelic army—is an extremely important company called the twenty-four elders. John's description of them gives us enough information to figure out who they are and the role they play in God's system.

First of all, we know these individuals carry great responsibility because they are the only beings that occupy thrones around the throne of God. John observes:

"Around the throne were twenty-four thrones, and on the thrones I saw twenty-four elders sitting, clothed in white robes; and they had crowns of gold on their heads" (Revelation 4:4).

The cherubim, the four living creatures, and all the angels *stand* around the throne of God, indicating their readiness for action. By contrast the twenty-four elders are *seated* in God's presence, indicating that they are dedicated to some ongoing throne-room proceedings in direct consultation with the Lord. But what proceedings?

Correlating John's vision in Revelation 4 and 5 with the vision of Daniel chapter 7, it becomes clear that the twenty-four elders preside as a kind of jury or as a set of witnesses in the event known in Scripture as *the judgment*. This means they are involved in the evaluation of individual human cases as their eternal destinies are decided.

John also indicates that the elders function in some kind of mediatory or priestly role. He says that they bow down "before the Lamb [Christ], each having a harp, and golden bowls full of incense, which are the prayers of the saints" (Revelation 5:8). Evidently, the twenty-four elders are not only participants in the judgment, but they are also engaged in the process by which prayers are answered.

The fact that the elders are twenty-four in number, coupled with the fact that they participate in the judgment and perform priestly duties, makes it easy for us to identify who they are as a group.

In the Old Testament system of priesthood, King David organized the workload into twenty-four cycles or shifts, designating twenty-four "officials of the sanctuary and officials of the house of God" (1 Chronicles 24:5; also see verse 18). This is the one and only interpretive correspondent in all of Scripture to the twenty-four elders in the book of Revelation. Whereas the Old Testament sanctuary and its priesthood were symbolic, what John saw in the heavenly realm reveals to us the fulfillment of those symbols. The twenty-four elders enthroned around God in heaven are the antitype or reality to which the twenty-four priestly officials of the Old Testament pointed.

Therefore, unlike the two covering cherubim, and unlike the four living creatures and the vast army of angels that surround God's throne, the twenty-four elders are not heavenly beings. They are, in fact, of earthly origin, which is to say, they are human beings and not of the angelic order. We know this to be the case, because, biblically speaking, only human beings qualify to occupy priestly roles. Paul explains in Hebrews that even Jesus Christ, the divine Son of God, became human so that we who are human could know Him as a sympathetic, understanding High Priest (Hebrews 4:14-16; 5:1-11). In Scripture, only humans can be priests on behalf of humans. Angels are never said to function in priestly capacities. Revelation 20:4-6 says that during the millennium the entire company of redeemed human beings will be seated on thrones, participate in the judgment, and be "priests of God." It is certain, then, that the twenty-four elders around the throne of God are a select group of human beings who are engaged with God in matters of mediation and judgment pertaining to the human race. Redeemed from among humanity, the twenty-four elders are busy examining the individual lives of those who yet remain on earth, watching, weighing, sympathizing, and bearing our prayers in "golden bowls," as it were, before the One who has power to orchestrate our every need.

The number twenty-four is itself significant. Twelve is the number that represents the people of God in the Old Testament, derived from the fact that Jacob had twelve sons who formed the twelve tribes of Israel. Twelve is also the number that represents the church of God in the New Testament, formed by the twelve apostles. The city of

God, the New Jerusalem, is said by John to have twelve foundations bearing the names of the twelve apostles, and twelve gates bearing the names of the twelve tribes of Israel (Revelation 21:12-14). The twelve tribes from the Old Testament and the twelve apostles from the New Testament together give us the number twenty-four and represent the redeemed of both eras. The symbolism of the double twelve, equaling twenty-four, indicates that the twenty-four elders are most likely twelve representatives from each biblical era. The Bible also indicates that a special resurrection occurred at the time of the resurrection of Jesus (Ephesians 4:8). It is likely that the twenty-four elders are composed of individuals from this resurrected company. Whoever they are by name, it is certain they are human beings and not angels or any other beings of heavenly origin.

The Worlds
This now brings us to what we will depict as circle seven.

Beyond the triune God, the two cherubim, the four living creatures, the twenty-four elders, and the two regiments of the angelic armies, there is one more orbiting circle of living beings that contributes to the formation of God's kingdom.

We will call the seventh circle, *The Worlds.*

Of course, we first think of our own world, Planet Earth with its human race. At some point after the creation of the angelic order, from within the inner circle of divine fellowship, one of the eternal three was heard to say, "Let Us make man in Our image, according to Our likeness" (Genesis 1:26).

But Scripture informs us that earth is not the only inhabited planet in the universe. Sometime along the way in the chronology of creation, God made other population centers. Non-human civilizations exist out there somewhere in the cosmos. Paul says that Christ "made the worlds" (Hebrews 1:2), plural. He could mean merely uninhabited planets like Venus and Mars, but this is unlikely the case when we take into account Paul's general conception of the cosmos at large. Elsewhere he speaks of "principalities and powers in heavenly places" or "rulers and authorities in the heavenly realms" (Ephesians 3:10, NKJV and NIV). It stands to reason that where there are rulers and authorities, there are also population groups that are organized under their leadership. Clearly Paul is describing inhabited realms.

The apostle John addresses the "heavens, and you who dwell in them," while declaring "woe to the inhabitants of the earth" (Revelation 12:12). And Isaiah cries out, "Hear, O heavens, and give ear, O earth!" (Isaiah 1:2). It is evident that the heavens are inhabited with rational beings that can be called upon to observe events transpiring on earth.

We are told in the book of Job that when the human race was being created, "the morning stars sang together, and all the sons of God shouted for joy" (Job 38:7). There are two categories of celestial beings mentioned here who witnessed the making of our world and therefore predate human existence. The symbolic term, "the stars of God," refers to a category of beings we are already familiar with. In the Bible stars are a metaphor for angels (Revelation 1:20; 12:4, 7-9). But who composes the second group of beings, the ones called "the sons of God," who rejoiced along with the angels at the creation of our world? Fortunately, we don't need to guess, because they are brought to view earlier in the story of Job.

"Now there was a day when the sons of God came to present themselves before the LORD, and Satan also came among them. And the LORD said to Satan, 'From where do you come?' So Satan answered the LORD and said, 'From going to and fro on the earth, and from walking back and forth on it'" (Job 1:6-7).

Apparently, God calls heavenly council meetings from time to time. On this particular occasion "the sons of God *came* to present themselves before the Lord." Unlike the angels, these particular beings do not dwell in God's immediate presence. They are called upon to *come* to meet with the Lord. Clearly, these "sons of God" reside elsewhere in God's universe and must travel in order to convene with Him in heavenly council sessions.

We also notice that when the "sons of God came to present themselves before the Lord," strangely enough, "Satan came also among them." God does not ask Satan *why* he feels the right to attend this meeting, but rather the Lord asks, "From *where* do you come?" This is a meeting of individuals who represent various territories in God's universe. Each one is there because of "*where*" they come from. So when Satan is asked *where* he comes from, it is a question regarding what territory he purports to represent. His answer is bold and revealing: "Earth."

The fact that Satan attended a meeting in which a group called "the sons of God" came from various regions of the universe to meet with the Lord, coupled with the fact that Satan claimed to be present in the meeting as the representative head of Earth, suggests that these sons of God were also present in the meeting as representative heads of their own respective worlds.

When the genealogy of Christ is mapped out in Luke's gospel, each person in the lineage is called the son of a particular human father: ". . . David, the son of Jesse, the son of Obed . . ." and so on. The naming of fathers and sons goes on like this until we at last read, "Adam, the son of God" (Luke 3:38). While every human being is a son or daughter of God by virtue of procreation, Adam was the son of God in a unique, primary sense. He was created by God first generation. Adam had no human parents. If Adam and Eve had never fallen prey to Satan's hostile takeover, Adam would have remained the representative head of Earth and its inhabitants. Now Satan claims that position.

We are rationally justified, then, in concluding that "the sons of God" who come from various territories of the universe to meet with God from time to time, and who watched with the angels as God created the human race, are to their own worlds what Adam was to ours, and what Satan now claims to be to ours. They are the representative heads of the populous areas that dot the cosmos, the "rulers and authorities" of the "heavenly realms" spoken of by Paul. Clearly, there are other inhabited worlds that contribute to the overall composition of God's vast kingdom.

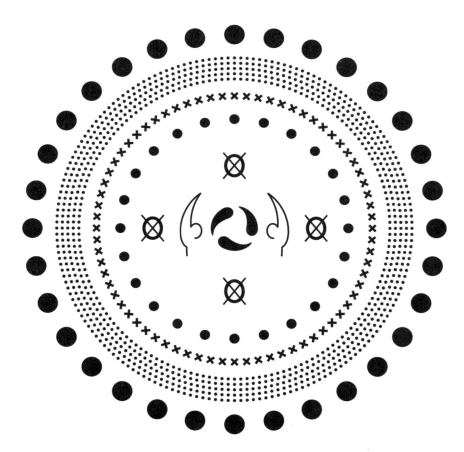

1. The Inner Circle: Father, Son and Holy Spirit.

2. Second Circle: The Two Covering Cherubim.

3. Third Circle: The Four Living Creatures.

4. Fourth Circle: The Twenty-Four Elders.

5. Fifth Circle: The Thousand Thousands.

6. Sixth Circle: The Ten Thousand Times Ten Thousand.

7. Seventh Circle: The Worlds.

Shape And Pattern

We have drawn upon the visions of four prophets to construct a model of God's kingdom, but no doubt the divine government is far more elaborate than has been revealed to us. I've only given here a childish sketch at best. My goal has not been to give a detailed blueprint of God's organizational structure (how could I?), but simply to call attention to its basic architectural form and the manner in which it operates: it is decidedly concentric and organized for out-reaching service. This is important to understand, because getting a sense of how the unfallen heavenly realm functions can serve to imprint a conception on our minds of the kind of person God is and the kind of people He is calling us to become preparatory to becoming citizens of His eternal kingdom.

We have seen that there are at least seven circles of outgoing action that compose God's government. Within the system we see leadership and service, delegation and autonomy, all operating as an other-centered stream of activity flowing from the inner circle of divine love. As odd as it may sound to our egocentric minds, God's kingdom is not essentially a hierarchical structure, but rather a concentric one. It's not a pyramid with God at the top dictating, but a series of rippling circles with God at the center as the greatest servant of all. God's ways and laws are so utterly foreign to our fallen natures that we can barely muster vocabulary to explain it to ourselves, nor are we inclined to believe it at first consideration. There is no existing governing model in our world to point at as an example of how a society would operate if ruled by love alone. We simply don't know what selflessness looks like until we really see and process the incarnation, life, and death of Jesus Christ. In Him we witness what love is and how it behaves. Looking to Christ it becomes evident that *love is power* from God's perspective. God lives in total non-concern for Himself in favor of others. The Creator is not primarily concerned with being in control, but with the free flow of rational, reciprocal love. He only exercises His power in a controlling capacity to the extent that we fail at the task of proper self-government, and even then the control He does exert is mostly by means of providential guidance, inner conviction, and angelic help, all calculated to arouse our own wills to free action. His ultimate goal is that all who live in His universe would be voluntarily governed by self-giving love.

In essence, what we've been talking about in this chapter is the shape of the unfallen realm of reality and the pattern in which it moves, taking its form from the shape and pattern of God's heart. And by logical extension we're also talking about the original shape of the human heart and the pattern in which it was designed to move. Human nature was made for self-giving motion, for service, for love. We only live as we were meant to live when we find our place in the concentric circles that emanate from the life-giving fire of divine love that rages at the center of the universe. The kingdom of God is a massive relational structure of love. We alone, the fallen human race, are out of sync with the way things are done in God's creation. The plan of salvation is the quest of heaven to reintegrate humanity into the social network of other-centered love that reigns supreme beyond our wounded world.

Now that we've constructed a basic understanding of God's character and kingdom, we are prepared to get a little more personal and a lot more practical.

six

S E X

A few years back a major Internet search engine noted that for a period of time there were two unexpected words running neck and neck, trading off first place back and forth as the top web search:

God and Sex.

No great surprise, really.

Even a casual glance at our world reveals that God and sex are the two highest-ranking human obsessions. After 150 years of Darwinian evolution building its case against God's existence, only about 800 million people claim to be atheists, leaving a whopping six billion people who still believe in some sort of deity.

For a while there were bumper stickers that said, "God is dead—*Nietzsche.*"

Now there are bumper stickers that say, "Nietzsche is dead—*God.*"

God is either a very persistent illusion, or a very persistent lover. And if a lover, sex is definitely in competition with the Lord for first place in human interest. But rather than ask whether God or sex has the lead in this odd race, there is a more interesting question to pose: What do God and sex have in common that they would both pull so profoundly and persistently on human beings?

Divine Plurality

"In the beginning God . . . " (Genesis 1:1).

That's how the Bible opens as the immediate prelude to human existence.

And to human sexuality.

In the original language the word is not "God," as though a generic deity is being introduced to us. Upon your first encounter with me I would not say, "Hi! I'm human." Rather, I'd tell you my name: "Hi! I'm Ty." I certainly am human, but I am a distinct and identifiable human, just as you are. As such, we each bear a name. The Bible opens by introducing to us a specific God with a specific identity and character. Therefore this God bears a name.

"In the beginning Elohim . . . "

There we go. Now we're getting acquainted.

God's name is Elohim. But this is no ordinary name. In fact, it's a peculiar kind of name, but also very enlightening. Peculiar, because it's a plural noun. Enlightening, because it contains the secret of God's essential identity, as well as the secret of the complex reality of human sexuality.

The name Elohim informs us that God is a plurality of being, not a singularity of being. Elohim, as a plural noun, would be like me introducing myself to you as "Tys." You'd be thinking one of two things: either, "Poor guy—he obviously does not understand how to make a proper use of English grammar," or, "Pity the delusional fellow—he thinks there's more than one of him." Either way, you would not take my plural introduction of myself seriously. I'm just one person and cannot justifiably bear a plural name.

But God can and does.

God is Elohim, because God is what we might call a plural singularity.

God is both self and other within the sacred parameters of the divine nature.

God is a social unit.

A relational complex.

A friendship.

An intimacy of other-centered, self-giving love.

And it is from the womb of this divine intimacy that "Elohim said, 'Let Us make humanity in Our image, according to Our likeness'. . . . So Elohim created humanity in His own image; in the image of Elohim He created him; male and female He created them" (Genesis 1:26-27, PT).

God is an "Us."

Not merely an "I" or a "Me," but an "Us."

So God's image is a "them."

In Scripture, God is defined as a personal being, not as an impersonal force; as a plural being, not as a solitary self; and as a passionate being, not as an impassible isolationist. God is a personal plural being of passionate, other-centered love.

It is natural, then, that when God made the first man He would say, "It is not good that man should be alone" (Genesis 2:18).

Why?

Because God is not alone, and humanity was created to be a replica of the divine image. So God said of the man, "I need to make a suitable partner for him" (Genesis 2:18, CEV). After making the woman, God "brought her to the man" (Genesis 2:22). What happened next is exactly what God planned: the two became "one flesh" (Genesis 2:24). The sexual relationship between the man and the woman was somehow expressive of the image of God, not the physical act itself, but the self-giving love it facilitated and expressed.

Theological Ramifications

Now we're beginning to see why God and sex hold such closely associated ground in the human experience. The sexual union between a man and a woman—even in its present severely broken and damaged state—speaks to us on a deep primal level of God's love. It is no trivial matter that in Scripture God repeatedly invokes the matrimonial union of a man and a woman as a metaphoric example of the relationship He desires with us (Ezekiel 16; Hosea 2; Ephesians 5; Revelation 19).

Human sexuality was designed by God, and was, therefore, patterned after something deeply rooted in the divine identity. That something is the self-giving, other-centered love that exists between the members of the Trinity. Is it any wonder, then, that human sexuality has been so deliberately malformed, perverted, and twisted into the ultimate act of anti-love self-gratification? If sex forms a spiritual passageway of understanding into deeper intimacy with God, it is not surprising that the adversary of both God and man, who stands in evil array against the atonement, would bend his powers to the task of making human sexuality a receptacle of profanity, lust, and shame.

Nothing hurts so bad, wounds so deep, nor confuses one's sense of self in relation to others so darkly as a violated sexuality. And no human relation holds more power to open the mind to the meaning of God's self-giving love, and to calibrate the soul for spiritual intercourse with its Maker, than does a beautiful sexual union within the sacred commitment of marriage.

In Ephesians 4:19, Paul explains that the human capacity for love is gradually lost through lust. He says we can come to the place where we are "past feeling" (NKJV), "having lost all sensitivity" (NIV). When that happens the appetite cannot be satisfied so we dive into "sensuality," only to experience its diminishing returns. Sensuality, or lust, is sexual gratification without love, self-focused sex, in which the other is related to as a tool or object used for pleasure as an end in itself without the faithfulness of lifelong commitment as the underlying meaning.

Paul further explains that lust is actuated by "greediness" (NKJV), from the Greek word *pleion*, which means *more*, as in *get more*. One Bible translation renders the word, "A continual lust for more" (NIV).

But here's the thing about greed, about living to get more:

There's never enough to satisfy.

Why?

Because *getting* can't satisfy.

Only *giving* can.

Lust is the ultimate illusion. It promises what it can't deliver. Getting more and more and more actually leads to having less and less and less. The very capacity for pleasure is eroded from the soul, until love itself is a mystery beyond comprehension or appreciation. What is it? We don't know anymore. And most frightening of all, we can come to the place where we don't even care. At that point, the Elohim image is gone from the fine mechanisms of our souls. That's where lust leads. And that's why if there is one aspect of human nature that should be guarded with superhero vigilance more than any other, it is our sexuality. There are many reasons to guard this sacred dimension of our lives with strict parameters of moral purity, but this one is at the top of the list.

The Severing

The etymology of the word "sex" is deeper than most of us know, and yet, we do know.

"Sex" is of Latin origin, from the word *secare*. It means "to sever, to amputate, to disconnect from the whole." Other related words are sect, section, dissect, bisect.

The sexual act involves a severing of one's self.

A dividing of one's self.

It involves giving yourself away.

We do know, don't we?

Each of us is a self-contained person. Our thoughts, our feelings, our motives, our desires, our deep inner personhood is all housed within the parameters of the individual person that each of us is. Then some *other* enters the picture, distinct in their influence over us from all the other others we have known.

What's happening to us?

We're falling in love.

More precisely, we are moving in the direction of potentially falling in love, which means someone is becoming in our eyes more important than ourselves. Our gaze, our interests, our energies are becoming centered elsewhere than on ourselves. All that we are as an individual begins to gravitate outward. We see and feel that certain someone in a way that is both threatening and promising. We find ourselves reaching out toward him, towards her, hoping that desire will meet desire and merge to form something new. We sense that some beautiful union is possible, and we are eager to dive in. We begin to experience their otherness and our own selfhood with acute awareness and intense attraction. That awareness of the other harkens back to when humanity once lived, like God lives, with complete other-centeredness. It is an echo of Eden. All Adam could see was Eve. All Eve could see was Adam. But that was before "the eyes of them both were opened, and they knew that they were naked" (Genesis 3:7), before the human gaze turned inward. Now we are deeply broken in our capacity for navigating the mystery of love. Nevertheless, the love we experience is reminiscent of the fact that we were psychologically engineered with the ability to think, feel, and act outside of the narrow confines of ourselves.

So we take the plunge.

We open ourselves up and give ourselves away.

We undergo the severing.

The sexual experience cuts into our bodies and into our souls deeper than any other experience. But the severing is not the whole meaning of sex. By implication, sex means to sever or divide one's self *into another*—to give part of one's self away to someone else. The severed self is not cast into a void. It's not severed to die, but rather to take on new life in union with the receiver, to form a new identity composed of two lovers who have now become one. A transaction has occurred. A deep exchange of self into self in both directions has now happened, and we will literally never be the same person again. In the most intimate sense, we carry in ourselves another person's love.

Atonement
It makes sense then that God would employ the sexual relation of man and woman as a window into the meaning of the atonement, He is seeking to achieve between Himself and humanity. Sex is the most profoundly intimate giving of self that we humans ever experience, at least it can be and it is meant to be.

The atonement is a spiritual reality that runs parallel in essential character to the sexual experience. Of course the atonement is not sex, but it is like sex in that it involves a deep giving of two selves into one another: the divine into the human, and the human into the divine.

In the spiritual realm, first God takes the initiative by giving the totality of Himself into humanity. In the incarnation of God in Christ, a severing of the divine self occurred. For love of you and me, the one who is "in very nature God" was voluntarily separated from the triune complex of divinity, taking the monumental step of condescending into human nature (Philippians 2:6, NIV).

The child grows into a man.

Jesus steps into the public eye to begin His ministry.

The religious people of the time expect the Messiah to wield military might, conquer the Romans, and exalt Israel to the pinnacle of political power. But contrary to these expectations, John the Baptist announces Jesus as "the Bridegroom" who has come to our world for marriage. Jesus is "the One to whom the bride belongs" (John 3:29, TEV).

The ministry of Jesus turns out to be a courting process. He is seeking to woo and win the human heart by His love. He is fulfilling the Old Testament prophecies about God planning to "allure" us and "betroth" us, because He sees that "the time has come for" us "to fall in love" (Hosea 2:14-21; Ezekiel 16:8). When Jesus speaks to the disciples about His death on the cross, He employs the language of love from the Song of Solomon. "Draw me away" (Song of Solomon 1:4), says Shulamite, giving voice to the universal human longing. "I, when I am lifted up, will draw all peoples to Me" (John 12:32, AB), Jesus responds. His self-sacrificing death on the cross is the epic demonstration of divine love.

The cross is set forth before our eyes to draw our hearts to "the Desire of all nations" (Haggai 2:7), because the cross is the severing of God, the complete giving of the divine self to humanity.

As Jesus approaches the end of the courtship process and is about to leave the world, He speaks in terms of preparing a place for us in His Father's house, which was the customary manner in which a man would prepare for his bride in Hebrew culture:

"In my Father's house are many rooms; if it were not so, I would have told you. I am going there to prepare a place for you. And if I go and prepare a place for you, I will come back and take you to be with Me" (John 14:2-4, NIV).

Jesus is unmistakably following the cultural pattern for obtaining a bride. A man who wanted to marry a woman would come to her home village. He would engage her in courtship. Once the matter was settled, he would depart from her for a time, back to his family, where he would build a room onto his father's house. In this way he would prepare a place for his bride. Then he would return to take her to their new home.

As Jesus comes to the end of His ministry, in His atonement prayer He calls into application the Hebrew language for sexual union in order to describe what He desires to accomplish in human salvation:

"This is eternal life," He prays, "that they may *know* You, the only true God, and Jesus Christ whom You have sent" (John 17:3). He is here drawing upon Genesis 4:1: "Adam *knew* Eve his wife, and she conceived." Then, utilizing the word for matrimonial union, He prays, "that they all may be *one,* as You, Father, are in Me, and I in You; that they also may be *one* in Us . . . just as We are *one:* I in them, and You in Me; that they may be made perfect in *one* . . . that the love with which You loved Me may be in them, and I in them" (John 17:21-23).

If human sexuality hails from the image of God, and if sex is, by definition, the severing of two selves into one another, then God must be an incredibly beautiful person after all. And He must be inviting us into something unimaginably glorious.

seven

P U R S U E D

aura Emily.

I've never known anyone so hungry for love and so relentless in its pursuit.

Almost suicidal.

She left home at the tender age of fourteen, lied about her age, got a job and began the hopeful and unexpectedly painful journey of giving her heart and body to one man after another, each time believing their words of commitment with a little less confidence, each time the hunger for love a little more suppressed, but each time somehow rising to try again.

When she was eighteen, Johnny came along. He was charismatic, charming, and believable. She said he opened her up like none of the guys before him, and many years later she said he was the only one she ever really loved. They say, whoever *they* are, that first loves are the deepest and make indelible cuts in the soul. I think the reason she loved him the way she did was because of me. I was the child of their passion, partly him, partly her. She told me one time that I reminded her of him, and I could tell that was a good thing.

But Johnny was a party boy and Laura Emily was now a mom. She was afraid. To her, Johnny was *the one*. To him, she was one among many. He had her heart, but from all I've been able to piece together, he didn't really want it. He just wanted to have a good time, and the whole baby thing was not his idea of fun.

So she gave him an ultimatum.

It was a desperate move. She thought he would choose her and his son. He didn't. She was proud enough and stubborn enough that she felt obligated to follow through on her threat to leave.

Love is like that.

It gets desperate, because it wants all or nothing.

So she left.

And she cried a lot for a long time.

Laura Emily never saw Johnny again. But her desire for love was unabated. She tried again and again.

There was the rock star roadie.

There was the older man who wanted a younger pretty girl at his side.

There was the big shot politician, who became the father of my next younger brother.

Then Charles came into her life. He swept her up into his complements, his obsessive attention, his contagious humor, and most of all his fun way with her boys. She was so sure he was the one, and she was so shocked when he hit her for the first of many times on their honeymoon night. She was afraid and trapped and soon the mother of four kids. She received her last beating one 4th of July. She escaped with her children late that night, never to return.

After beginning life as a single mom of four, her hunger for love continued. Next was the pilot of the Goodyear Blimp. After taking a fun ride in the big flying advertisement, I asked my mom, "Is that man going to be our new dad?" She said, "Maybe. I'm not sure." Soon he stopped coming around. She cried.

Then there was the younger man, the cool surfer guy, Rick. He was the older brother of my two best friends at the time, the twins, Stan and Harold. At first she was pretty sure this was the man of her dreams. He wasn't. He was more like the man of her nightmares. Once he started becoming abusive, she told him to get lost, but he kept coming over and making promises and threats. Mostly threats. Sometimes he would break in and be sitting there when I'd come home from school.

Finally, still in her early 30s, a guy named Allen entered the picture. I think he scared off the young surfer dude. Allen was a sight to behold, a Robert Redford look alike, only a lot more muscles. He looked much more dangerous than Robert Redford. He was an ex-biker from the Misfits biker gang. To this day I don't think I've ever met a more charming, likeable guy, as far as sheer personality goes. Despite his tendency to beat people up in public, he treated Laura Emily like a queen. She was so happy with him.

But then, unexpectedly, her story went in a whole new direction.

Laura Emily met another man, a man of an entirely different character and involving an entirely different kind of attraction. She claimed that the love she had been looking for all her life was now found in the man, Jesus Christ. And she claimed that this man was none other than God Himself in human flesh. Outrageous, I know. But that's what she believed.

Allen thought she had lost her mind, because according to him it was far more likely that Planet Earth had been seeded by aliens and that that's where we humans came from. I thought she had lost it too, although I wasn't fond of the alien hypothesis either. As the eldest of four kids I tried to assure my younger siblings that mom would recover from her religious lunacy. She didn't. At first, I thought she seemed like a totally different person and it made me angry. But then I realized she was like a better version of herself.

Allen began saying she had to choose between him and this Jesus thing. She kept choosing both, insisting that there was no conflict between the two commitments. She said she could love him and Jesus. He didn't think so. One day he left for work and never returned.

Her heart was broken again, and yet this time, strangely whole for the first time, because now her field of vision was shifted a full 180 degrees. Laura Emily, the relentless pursuer of love, now realized that she was herself being pursued by a greater love than she had ever known. Longing for love, she was all along the object of a love that lay behind, behind and yet further behind every broken fragment of human love. Her desire for trust and loyalty and friendship was now seen to be the echo of her Creator's desire for her trust and loyalty and friendship. Desire had now met its source and its object.

The Chase

What if your strongest yearnings, like Laura Emily's, are for a love that cannot find a perfect match in this world?

What if you, too, are the object of an unstoppable pursuer's ingenious orchestrations and providential arrangements?

According to the God of the Bible, you are.

It is in the very nature of His love to chase you down with a relentless passion that knows no end short of complete self-sacrifice.

David grasped the pursuing dimension of God's love. In his most famous song, the poet-king of Israel envisioned the sovereign God of the universe as a Shepherd, not only caring for His sheep when they are in the fold, but running after them when they wander away:

"The LORD is my shepherd, I shall not be in want. He makes me lie down in green pastures, He leads me beside quiet waters, He restores my soul. He guides me in paths of righteousness for His name's sake. Even though I walk through the valley of the shadow of death, I will fear no evil, for You are with me; Your rod and your staff, they comfort me. You prepare a table before me in the presence of my enemies. You anoint my head with oil; my cup overflows. Surely goodness and love will follow me all the days of my life, and I will dwell in the house of the LORD forever" (Psalm 23, NIV).

It's that last line we need to especially notice at this juncture of our journey together.

"Surely goodness and love will follow me all the days of my life."

A specifically Jewish translation says,

"Only goodness and steadfast love shall pursue me all the days of my life" (PTH).

One of the distinctive features of divine love is that it takes aggressive action to pursue the object of its desire. And you and I just happen to be that object!

Conversely, one of the biggest misconceptions about God that overshadows our world is the idea that God must be pursued and found by human beings,

that we are more interested in Him than He is in us,

that His interest must be aroused by our overtures, placations, or worthy deeds, that He is aloof, distant, even cold, and must be searched out and worked upon in order that His favor might be secured.

Nothing could be further from the truth.

Building upon David's song, Jesus portrayed God as a searching Shepherd venturing into perilous territory to rescue even one lost sheep (Luke 15:4-7). This is God Himself telling us that He will go to any extreme necessary to save us, even one of us.

Peter picks up the Shepherd metaphor and constructs deep and meaningful theology around it. He says that God "Himself bore our sins in His own body on the tree, that we, having died to sins, might live for righteousness—by whose stripes we are healed. For you were like sheep going astray, but have now returned to the Shepherd and Overseer of your souls" (1 Peter 2:24-25).

Peter would have us understand that the cause of the broken relationship lies in us, not in God. We are like sheep gone astray. God's response, however, is anything but passive. He chases after us into perilous territory, not on the physical terrain, but into the perilous psychological territory of our sin and all the horrific shame it entails. This is what Peter means when he says that Jesus "bore our sins." He owned them as if they belonged to Him, enduring in Himself the full-blown reality of our guilt. Embracing the death we had earned, He drank down into His soul the just punishment we deserved. And He did all this, Peter explains, so that we might be moved by His love to return to the Shepherd and Overseer of our souls.

Don't miss the correlation between Shepherd and *Overseer*.

The word Peter uses here, *episkopos*, contains fabulous insight to the character of God. It is a construction of two Greek words: *epi*, which means to be so close as to be superimposed, and *skopos*, which means to watch or give attentiveness to. Peter wants us to picture God hovering over our souls with a watchfulness so attentive that it is as if He is superimposed over us. In other words, micro close! He is hyperaware of our every intellectual movement and of our every emotional impulse.

The Quenching

I know what Jesus would have said to Laura Emily if He had lived in her day, because He met a similar woman is His day. She is often referred to as "the woman at the well." Her story is recorded in John 4. Jesus encountered her after her life had taken many twists and turns. A history had been written in her soul, not too dissimilar to your history and mine in basic substance, and very similar to the history of Laura Emily.

Jesus could see that history on her face, in her eyes, and in the way she carried herself. She was insecure and off-putting, even diversionary. When Jesus tried to get real with her she tried to get theological with Him, attempting to turn the conversation to issues of religious debate.

Theological controversy is often a great place to hide from God.

"Give me a drink," Jesus says.

She is shocked at His lack of cultural prejudice.

"How is it that You, being a Jew, ask a drink from me, a Samaritan woman?"

She lives under a double rejection: she is a Samaritan and a woman. But actually, there is a third and deeper sense of rejection she is bearing, and that's where Jesus is trying to penetrate. He and the woman proceed to engage in a metaphoric exchange and they both know what they're really talking about.

Jesus says to her, "If you knew the gift of God, and who it is who says to you, 'Give Me a drink,' you would have asked Him, and He would have given you living water."

Here Jesus is diagnosing the human predicament. He recognizes that what we really want lies in Him. He knows that beneath our surface pursuits we actually desire a substantial relational love only to be found in Him. And He discerns that if we knew Him to be the source of that love, we would ask Him for it. The woman is quick to follow His lead. Thirsty people are like that. They follow the scent of water.

"Where then do You get that living water?"

She wants to know. The prospect is tantalizing, hopeful, too good to be true.

Jesus doesn't immediately divulge the source of the quenching He is offering her. First, He further arouses her desire for it.

"Whoever drinks of this [literal] water will thirst again, but whoever drinks of the water that I shall give him will never thirst. But the water that I shall give him will become in him a fountain of water springing up into everlasting life."

What a startling and alluring claim!

Jesus offers some kind of something, symbolized by water, that He says will quench her thirst so deeply and completely that she will never thirst again. What He has to give her, and to us, is the exact match to the deepest desire that courses through our souls. And if that's not enough, the infilling He offers is of such a character that it will more than satisfy our own need. It will spring up out of us like a fountain of life to others. It's a kind of satisfaction that will make us givers, rather than merely receivers.

The woman at the well responds with no-nonsense urgency, "Sir, give me this water, that I may not thirst."

But Jesus probes deeper still. He wants her to feel her need with a heightened sense of awareness, to see it for what it really is, to define it in relation to her life's history and her failed pursuits. So He brings up the most sensitive subject in her life, because the most sensitive areas of our lives are the secret places of our deepest desires.

She says, "Sir, give me this water."

And Jesus responds, "Go, call your husband, and come here."

Huh?

What's my husband got to do with it?

Of course the answer is, *Everything*!

She immediately tries to evade the sensitive topic and keep her history buried. "I have no husband," she states with finality, offering not another word. End of subject! But that's not the end of the subject. In fact, that *is* the subject. The truth is hiding in plain sight in her relational escapades. Now it's beginning to become clear what kind of thirst-quenching Jesus has in mind. It is decidedly relational in nature and has to do with matters of intimacy.

She's not telling Jesus anything He doesn't already know.

"You have well said, 'I have no husband,' for you have had five husbands, and the one whom you now have is not your husband."

Boom!

On goes the light.

Imagine what she's thinking, what she's feeling, in this moment.

In a single casual sentence He just brought up to the surface years of painful history she would rather forget. And yet, Jesus knows this is where her desire for Him is most vividly manifested. He's not trying to hurt her, but rather to heal her, but to do so He must save her out of failed love into true love.

Look at yourself, He seems to be saying. *Your life is a series of repeated attempts at love. This reveals something. Your desire is good, but your aim is off. Here, allow Me to introduce to you the love you're really looking for.*

Jesus looks straight into this woman's sin and then straight past it, past her numerous failed relationships, because behind it all He discerns a longing for love . . .

a longing for love misguided,

a longing for love corrupted by selfishness and lust,

but a longing for love nonetheless.

The memories are too painful, and the fact that this man knows everything about her is more than she can bear. So she runs, not physically, but emotionally.

"Sir," she says with a labored casual poise, "I perceive that You are a prophet. Our fathers worshiped on this mountain, and you Jews say that in Jerusalem is the place where men ought to worship."

She tries to divert His gaze from her failures to a current point of religious debate. It doesn't work. He simply employs the hot topic to continue on with the personal topic.

"Woman, believe Me, the hour is coming when you will neither on this mountain, nor in Jerusalem, worship the Father. . . . But the hour is coming, and now is, when the true worshipers will worship the Father in spirit and in truth; for the Father is seeking such to worship Him."

Geography isn't the issue.

Psychology is . . . or *heartology.*

Whether we connect with God on this mountain or that one isn't the point, because our relationship with God isn't merely an external matter of form and cultural compliance. The real issue has to do with what we believe about God—is it the truth?—and how we feel about God—do we worship Him deep in our inmost being, in our spirit?

Honesty is the precursor to intimacy. God is seeking a particular kind of worshiper—those who worship in spirit and in truth, those who know God as He really is and genuinely love Him with their whole heart.

Jesus essentially tells the woman that she is seeking true love and so is God, making them a perfect match. She makes a tentative attempt to remain ambivalent, but the attraction she feels is so strong she has a hunch this is no ordinary man.

"I know that Messiah is coming (who is called Christ). When He comes, He will tell us all things."

Jesus responds, "I who speak to you am He."

Surprise!

Pleased to meet you!

You know this God I've been telling you about, the One who's looking for heartfelt, truth-believing worshipers? Well, I'm Him. And that water that forever satisfies the thirst of the soul, well, I'm that water. In all those relationships with all those men, you were looking for My love, and here I am looking for you.

A few months after the ex-biker left her, Laura Emily was diagnosed with cancer. Her life ended far too soon at the young age of 42. I miss her a lot. But I am happy to tell you that she died in love with the man of her dreams, who just happened to be the God of her deepest heart's desire.

May she rest in peace and meet the Lover of her soul face to face on resurrection morning.

I know she will.

eight

THINK, FEEL, DO

O n one of my international trips I found myself in close proximity to an odd cultural norm—odd only to me of course. As a guest in the home of a lovely family, I had just finished joining them for an excellent meal. There were six people at the table. Suddenly, the man at the head of the table let out a fully audible burp. And I mean audible. It had the clarity of a BOSE surround-sound speaker system. I immediately felt embarrassed for him, assuming it was an accidental emission.

But then another person burped, and another, and another, until all of them had done so and all eyes were on me. All at once it dawned on me that this was a completely acceptable table manner and was the customary method of expressing to the cook that the meal was enjoyed and appreciated. It was obvious that I was now expected to offer my own approving burp. I must say, the peer pressure was intense. But I honestly did not have one to offer, even after shyly covering my mouth and trying to create one. So I simply smiled and said, "Wow, that was delicious. Thank you!" This didn't seem to have the same level of authenticity as the burps did. I am sure if I had grown up in that culture I would have been as free with my burps as everyone else at the table were with theirs.

Certainly you've noticed that human behaviors are catchy and often even pandemic. We all so naturally mimic and copy one another.

This is why everyone in Canada says "eh" at the end of sentences, and why everyone in California says, "like," as in, "I was like, no way, really," and why everyone in New York says, "Ya know what I mean?"

This is why most Southerners just happen to have a Southern accent, and why scarely anyone in the Northwest has any accent at all.

This is why bell-bottoms come and go, and why back in 1939 men's undershirt sales dropped off after the movie *Gone With The Wind* became popular. The leading man, Clark Gable, was wearing a blousy shirt with three buttons opened revealing no undershirt, becoming the new definition of "cool."

This is why when the movie *Finding Nemo* came out, countless kids across the nation were flushing their family's aquarium fish down the toilet, hoping they would be reunited with their loved ones in the ocean.

It's not by accident that we're all so impressionable, so susceptible to one another's influence, and so uncannily like the people we hang around. There is a reason why we're all so inclined to integrate one another's personality and character traits into our own. It goes back to how we were made to begin with.

Cross-pollination

Human nature was originally designed for social integration and reciprocal reflection. We were made to feed on one another's love and virtue. God specifically engineered the inner workings of our minds for continual growth in personality and character. And He built into our natures an ingenious way for this to happen. We were to soar in non-stop mental, emotional and relational development through contact with one another. It was the divine intent that this growth would occur within the social process as we would receive one another's love in its many forms of personalized expression and then, having been enriched, reflect our continually enlarging love out to others.

Love is composed first of the ability to see others without reference to one's self, without consideration for benefit to one's self. Then, in the process of genuinely seeing and experiencing others, love responds by giving into the lives of others in the form of words, attitudes, and deeds of service. In each episode of any two individuals knowing and serving one another, a totally unique cross-pollination of character happens that makes each one more than they were before. A mutual enrichment of mind and heart occurs. Each one is enlarged in their identities and in their capacity for love.

Love is the infinite more. It's the only commodity in circulation that increases with expenditure. Love has no cap, no plateau, no that's-all-there-is stagnation point. It is the exhaustless ocean of meaning we move into as we move toward one another with selfless interest. No matter how mature a person's love may be, it is always possible to love more intelligently, more sensitively, more passionately. The reason for this is, quite simply, because God is love, which means love has an infinite capacity for configuration, application, creativity, and expression, in as much as God is infinite.

Think of the various people you know. You will notice that human character and personality is capable of manifesting itself in a countless array of little beauties and wonders, and big ones too. Think of *her* laughter, *his* facial expressions, *her* way of expressing gratitude with that certain flash of her eyes, *his* way of manifesting acceptance with his signature body language. Think of that special feeling of confidence *she* somehow has a way of arousing in you, and that incredible sense of affirmation *he* is able to ignite in you. Each person is totally original in the way they process and express love.

What We're Made Of

Each person, with all their delightful traits (for the sake of clarity we're ignoring the annoying traits at the moment), is a composite of the sum total of interactions they have had with others. I am what I am because of the string of social contacts I've had, and the same is true of you. Each unique individual is literally a pool of what they have seen and experienced in their interactions with family members and friends. All of those social interactions have resulted in the formation of a character and personality as singular as their fingerprint. Everyone is uncannily similar to others and yet totally unique. It's like chaos theory at its best—an endlessly emerging array of unpredictable and completely distinctive configurations of beauty.

That's how human nature and human society was designed by our Maker to function.

Now imagine the phenomenon of character cross-pollination happening without the presence of self-centeredness in any heart— each person thinking, feeling, and living without any egocentric sense about them, and totally outward in their frame of reference. Imagine an entire world of people living in other-centered social interaction. What would transpire?

A gorgeous interplay of personality,

a brilliant exchange of character traits,

a spectacular reciprocation of love,

moment by moment resulting in countless, ever new personalized expressions of the corporate human beauty,

each one incorporating the qualities of the others into their own character,

creating an eternally enlarging revelation of the One who is the infinite source of it all.

That was God's original plan. And that's why we're all such social sponges and reflectors. All the mimicking and copying we see in our world never would have been a problem if the Fall had never occurred. There would have been no bad traits of character to pick up, but only good ones. Whereas, in our current fallen world the reflective design of our natures is often to our detriment, in a sinless social structure it would have been to our eternal development.

The Law Of Beholding

By God's design we're all governed by a psychological law that is deeply inscribed in our natures. We can call it *The Law of Beholding*, following Paul's language (2 Corinthians 3:18), or *The Law of Reflection*, or *The Transforming Power of Belief.* Whatever we call it, the basic reality is that we tend to do what we see, or more precisely, we do what we believe. The beliefs we hold form the way we feel, and the way we feel dictates the way we behave.

As the law of gravity states, *what goes up must come down*, so the law of beholding states, *what goes in will come out.* Solomon articulated the matter nicely when he said, "As [a man] thinks in his heart, so is he" (Proverbs 23:7). This is the predominant, unswerving spiritual law continually operable in human nature.

Our thoughts (the things we believe to be true and of highest value)

shape our feelings (emotions, sentiments, intuitions and motives),

which dictate our behavior patterns (the way we relate to others).

There is vital cause-and-effect linkage between our thoughts, feelings and deeds.

The Power Of Belief

What we're talking about here is the power of belief to shape character. It is the submission of the mind to belief that exerts influence over our behavior.

Just how powerful is belief?

Consider a few cases brought to our attention by Dr. Herbert Benson, associate professor of medicine at Harvard Medical School, in his book, *Timeless Healing: The Power and Biology of Belief.*

By the subtitle of the book it is evident that Dr. Benson's thesis is that belief is such a powerful mechanism in the human experience that it can literally affect our physical health. First, Dr. Benson calls our attention to an ancient observation made by Hippocrates, the father of Western medicine:

"Some patients, though conscious that their condition is perilous, recover their health simply through their contentment with the goodness of the physician" (p. 35).

Hippocrates is here describing what would later be named "the placebo effect." The word "*placebo*" is from a Latin root that means, "I shall be pleasing or acceptable," or in its application to health, "I shall be well." The placebo effect occurs when a person suffering some adverse ailment has sufficient belief in the physician that their body actually heals itself in accordance with the physician's positive claim that healing will result from a remedy that actually has no healing power at all. The adverse symptoms vanish, not because the prescribed remedy had any effect, but because the patient believes the physician. In other words, belief is powerful enough to alter our biological condition for the better.

But the placebo effect has a negative counterpart phenomenon called, "the nocebo effect." Dr. Benson states:

"You see, belief can also work against us. The brain/body does digest unpleasant images and can fulfill ugly prophecies. Consider how often crime victims die from heart attacks, brought on not by any injuries but from the horror of being assaulted. Confirming this, one investigator autopsied such victims and observed that in eleven of fifteen cases there were no internal injuries. Instead, their deaths were caused by severe heart muscle damage called myofibrillar degeneration. Jolted by believing in a life-threatening danger, the body sustained this damage, releasing excessive amounts of the stress-relieving hormone norepinephrine, also called noradrenaline. A massive overdose of norepinephrine triggers a chain of biochemical events, often causing death" (p. 39).

Dr. Benson describes the placebo effect and the nocebo effect as "the materialization of beliefs into physical signs," citing the fact that "episodes of anger and hostility can translate into stomach ulcers and heart attacks." He speaks of "the vast interrelatedness of mind and body" and "how intimately our thoughts are related to our bodies" (p. 39).

So powerful is belief that a person who either intensely fears or desires pregnancy can experience all the physical signs of pregnancy without being pregnant.

"This phenomenon is called pseudocyesis (or pseudopregnancy) and is often considered 'the oldest known psychosomatic condition.' Hippocrates reported twelve cases of women 'who imagine they are pregnant seeing the menses are suppressed and the matrices swollen.' In the sixteenth century, Mary of Tudor, the Queen of England, experienced pseudocyesis several times with symptoms of pregnancy that spanned nine months and culminated in two episodes of false labor" (p. 43).

In modern documented cases of false pregnancy, physicians have reported that "menstruation stops and abdominal swelling occurs at a rate similar to that of a normal pregnancy. Breasts grow larger and more tender, and nipples change pigment as is consistent with pregnancy. Nipples also increase in size and milk is secreted. Some women feel what they think is fetal movement during the fourth or fifth month of false pregnancy. Dr. James A. Knight of Baylor

University reported that one man had a false pregnancy as well" (p. 44).

Now when a guy gets "pregnant," but isn't, you know the mind exerts a powerful effect on the body.

Benson concludes that, "The body does respond to the cravings of the soul, sometimes in dramatic ways, other times subtly" (p. 44).

But our thoughts are even more powerful still.

My thesis in this chapter is not a physiologic one, but a spiritual one. Not only do our thoughts and feelings impact our physical state of health, even more profound is the fact that our thoughts and feelings impact our very identities as human beings. Character, personality, and behavior patterns are shaped by what we believe. Human identity is malleable. Every moment of the day our characters are under construction. We are constantly undergoing a *becoming* process. And belief, or faith, is the primary mechanism by which we become who we are. Our characters are transformed by what we believe to be true about God.

The apostle Paul states:

"We all, with unveiled face, beholding as in a mirror the glory of the Lord, are being transformed into the same image from glory to glory" (2 Corinthians 3:18).

The "beholding" action of which Paul here speaks refers to the mental process of examining, contemplating, and perceiving. By the term, "the glory of the Lord," Paul means the character of God or the attributes that compose the divine identity. The word "transformed" is *metamorphosis* in the Greek. Anciently, the word referred to the dramatic recreation process a caterpillar undergoes in the cocoon so that it can emerge as a beautiful butterfly. Paul's take-home message is this:

By engaging the mind in the process of coming to know the truth about God's character, we will become changed into the same likeness. We reflect what we believe to be true about God.

Jesus spoke much regarding the fact that what we believe about God shapes who we are. First describing His own experience as a human being, He said, "Most assuredly, I say to you, the Son can do nothing of Himself, but what He sees the Father do; for whatever He does, the Son also does in like manner" (John 5:19).

We note here the vital relation between *seeing* and *doing*. What I *see*, I *do*, Jesus says. His usage of the word "see" is not a reference to literal eyesight, of course, but rather to perception. He means, what I *know* to be true about the Father determines how I *act* toward you. There is a direct line of experiential outcome from perception to behavior. Perception is the cause while behavior is the effect.

Jesus later explained that the transformative power of belief works in the negative direction as well:

"'I speak what I have seen with My Father, and you do what you have seen with your father . . . You do the deeds of your father. Then they said to Him . . . 'we have one Father—God.' Jesus said to them, 'If God were your Father, you would love Me, for I proceeded forth and came from God . . . you are of your father the devil, and the desires of your father you want to do'" (John 8:38-44).

Jesus is here speaking to the religious leaders of His day. He tells them that the way they are *behaving* toward Him flows directly out of what they *believe* about God. To their shock, He says that they are worshipers of the devil while thinking they are worshipers of God. Their murderous intent reveals that they don't know God's true character. They were attributing to God traits that really belong to the devil, and in so doing, they were deifying the character of Satan as if it were the character of God. In their hard, cold, condemnatory religion they were simply acting out their malformed picture of God.

The apostle John observes:

"He who does good is of God, but he who does evil has not seen God" (3 John 1:11).

Note again the connection between what one *sees* and what one *does*. John says that those who do evil do so because they have not seen God—they do not know God as He is. They are living out the deceptions they believe.

In fact, the entirety of human history has been corporately shaped by what is believed about God. The Bible traces all the woes of humanity back to a fundamental change of belief, resulting in a changed emotional state, resulting in actions of rebellion against God. All of the selfishness, greed, and broken vows; all of the hatred, violence, and war; all of the pain and suffering that accrues from all our anti-love behaviors—it's all simply the acting out of a deeply deceived sense of who God is and who we are in relation to Him. We've been lied to, and we're living out the lie.

The Primal Lie

According to the biblical record, the temptation and fall of humanity in Eden occurred first at the *thought,* or *belief,* level. Satan, the fallen angel formerly known as Lucifer, persuaded the father and mother of the human race to believe a picture of God that could not sustain love and trust. He slipped into their minds a complex of falsehood regarding the character of God, and our sordid history is the result.

Genesis 3:1-5 records the essential contents of the deception. Satan basically told humanity, *God is restricting your liberty and holding you under His dominance. He has lied to you about the result of asserting your freedom. You will not die as He has threatened. And God has a motive for all this control and deception. He knows that the moment you assert your freedom you'll be exalted to equality with Him, and He doesn't want that. He's looking out for Himself, not for you. God is self-serving, and you better live for yourself, too, if you want to soar to the higher plane He's keeping you from.*

Here was a subtle but effective attack on the very idea that "God is love." Satan achieved the Fall of mankind by capitalizing on the fact that what we believe about God dictates how we feel about God, which in turn dictates how we act toward God. So he attacked Adam and

Eve at the level of their thoughts. He told them lies about the character of God, which, when they believed them, distorted their perception of God, broke their trust toward Him, and drove them into rebellion. The deceiver essentially fabricated a complete inversion of reality in the human mind. By painting the Creator as self-serving, he turned the human focus inward on itself, arousing fear and generating feelings of self-preservation, which is the only option in a universe thought to be loveless. To know and believe that God is love was vitally necessary to the human continuation in love. Once the vision of God's self-giving love was removed from their hearts, the only direction they could go was to begin living for self in harmony with the falsehood they now believed. By beholding they had become changed, and we are their posterity.

We are now living in the psychological, emotional, and moral aftermath of the alternate view of reality Satan sold to humanity in Eden. Because we are a corporate body of reflectors, we all carry inborn distortions about God as a legacy from the Fall. Those distortions are magnified in us individually to the degree that we carry shame, which acts as a lens to further distort our perceptions of God. Those distortions are magnified yet further to the degree that we have been educated in false theologies.

Human nature was corrupted at its most foundational level—at the level of our beliefs about God. It is evident, therefore, that there can be only one possible way of restoration, salvation, and healing. We must come to know and believe the truth about God once more, which is exactly the task of the chapters that follow.

n i n e

E S S E N C E

*G*od is far more desirable than our darkened hearts know. You'll see what I mean as we begin now to make the most massively important and totally exciting discovery ever.

No exaggeration!

Student of Socrates, teacher of Aristotle, Plato was the man in the middle of the three "great" Greek philosophers.

Plato was known to his world as a thinker. Not in the sense that he was inclined to chase intellectual rabbits. He wasn't a recreational thinker, but an intentional, disciplined thinker with a very specific aim. A number of his beliefs were way ahead of his time, some were erroneous, and some downright horrific, but his idea about getting at the heart of a matter is very helpful. The big goal in his thinking enterprise was to peel back the surface layers and discover the foundation of a select list of concepts he regarded as vital.

What is the essence of truth?

The essence of goodness?

Of beauty?

Justice?

Citizenship?

Plato asked questions about *essence*, and these are some of the words he regarded as important. Convinced that words are packed with conceptual wealth and must be mined for the larger picture they can paint on our awareness, he specialized in cultivating the minds of his students in the art of defining what things mean. He worked from the premise that words are the building materials for ideas, and that every word is traceable to an *essential* meaning, that every word has a core concept within it. He believed that if one could define the essence of key words, one could begin to really grasp the contents of reality.

Words are like that. They are the abiding place of meaning. As such, they are extremely powerful. In this chapter, I would like explore with you the key word in the Old Testament Scriptures that defines the essence of God's character. This word distinguishes the God of the Hebrew patriarchs and prophets from all other conceptions of God in history (1 Kings 8:23). It's more of a comprehensive concept or a full-orbed vision of God's character than merely a word, but the single word contains the essence of the idea. In our quest to know what lies within the deep interior of God's identity, this particular word holds massive explanatory power. To know this word is to know who God is at heart.

Hesed.

As the Hebrew prophets endeavored to describe God and reach out to Him, hesed is the word they employed more frequently than any other, often coupling it with other words in an effort to expand its rich meaning. It is the best idea about God ever conceived, and the only attractive view of God humans have ever known among our world's plethora of religions. It is the only view of God that actually generates in the believer voluntary attraction toward God and leaves the soul unforced and free. All other pictures of God exert pressure, apply coercion, and manipulate the emotions without engaging the intellect. But the hesed picture of God motivates a freely rendered, intelligently conceived, and emotionally rich worship. According to *Strong's* Hebrew dictionary, hesed means "desire or ardour." It is the word that conveys God's full-throttle desire for you and me.

In the most definitive sense, hesed is *the* truth about God, the core essence of His being. All other divine attributes can be said to be expressions of hesed. You'll see what I mean as we progress.

A Personal Introduction

The hesed view of God's character was not merely conceived in the human imagination. Nobody made this up. Rather, it was revealed in the form of a personal introduction. In a world pervaded by arbitrary, appeasable "gods," a certain man heard a voice promising blessing and faithfulness *from* God *to* man (Genesis 12-22). And to the utter astonishment of the man, and all who would follow after him, it was the voice of God Himself making the promise. The man was known to his family as Abram, but God would eventually change his name to "Abraham." The name change would be made once his perception of God was altered sufficiently for the new name to be fitting.

In that epic divine-human encounter, a massive paradigm shift was to be set in motion, eventually to make a complete 180-degree rotation in the ultimate son of Abraham, Jesus Christ (John 8:54-58; Matthew 1:1), who would come to our world as the hesed of God incarnate.

Here was a God who was communicating to humanity, making promises, seeking covenant relationship, vowing Himself to be just and true in all His ways, and promising to create the same kind of character in all who would open their hearts to Him.

More than all that, here was a God who was promising to one day show up in the flesh to act out His faithful love to the point of giving His life for the world. This God would give Himself *as* the sacrifice for human salvation rather than require that sacrifice be offered by humanity to Him.

The God of Abraham bears no resemblance whatsoever to any of the gods popularly worshiped by the surrounding nations of the era or, for that matter, to any other worship system in history. To this day, the God of the ancient Hebrew people is the only promise-making, relationally conceived God to ever grace human awareness. That fact alone bears witness to the fact that this is the one and only true God.

Seeking to wrap their minds around the character of the divine personage who entered into the relationship with Abraham, the prophets either coined the word hesed or co-opted it from their existing cultural vocabulary and infused it with an enlarged divine meaning according to the truth they were encountering in God. Hesed came to undergird the entire ancient Hebrew view of God. It is a vision of unparalleled beauty.

Twenty-six To One

Hesed came to have such enormous meaning and conceptual content for the prophets that translators have struggled to limit themselves to any single English equivalent. In various Bible translations we find hesed rendered as:

Mercy

Unfailing love

Steadfast love

Faithful love

Lovingkindness

All of these translations are helpful and all of them leave yet more to
be understood. One scholar suggested to me that hesed is so large
with meaning that it would require 26 different English words to
adequately encompass its richness in Hebrew thought. He didn't
name the 26 words he had in mind, and it may have been an
arbitrarily chosen number to make a point. But I have come up with
my own list after surveying hesed's usage throughout the Hebrew
Bible. Hesed means God is characterized by:

Faithfulness

Mercy

Compassion

Changelessness

Determination

Constancy

Reliability

Commitment

Dependability

Predictability

Trustworthiness

Integrity

Patience

Hope

Devotion

Passion

Longsuffering

Justice

Truthfulness

Goodness

Kindness

Grace

Loyalty

Generosity

Faith

It's all there as you read the breathtaking story from Genesis to Revelation. Who could possibly not long for and worship a God like that? If such a God does rule the universe, can you image any more desirable prospect than to know this God?

A God Of Covenant

The overall idea of hesed is that the one and only true God is a God of *covenant*, a God who makes and keeps promises with unswerving integrity and reliability, and a God who maintains merciful loyalty even in the face of our failure to keep covenant with Him. Hesed says that God is intrinsically righteous, good, and true in Himself. His faithfulness is not conditioned by or contingent upon ours.

At the core of God's covenantal faithfulness is, remarkably, the pledge of Himself. Hesed is the biblical word for God's devotion to us at any cost to Himself. Because God *is* hesed at heart, the cross was inevitable for Him from the beginning. He knew that the moment we would exist He would love us above and before Himself. As soon as we were created, our Maker was forever pledged to us to the death.

This is the divine identity.

And this is the most astounding truth imaginable.

Currently, in the context of the Fall of humanity, hesed is the special or unique kind of love that exists in God for mankind but, in fact, it was never supposed to be unique to the way God lives. We were made in the image of God, and therefore we were made for the same kind of love. Hesed was supposed to be pervasive throughout creation. In the larger context of God's original plan, hesed is the very definition of *normality* for all free beings. The designed state of man—the normative condition for all autonomous creatures—is other-centered love, relational faithfulness, and self-giving devotion. It was God's intent that this kind of love (and this is the only thing that can rightfully be called *love*) would be the only actuating motive in every thought, feeling, and deed in every relationship. This is why sin is called "transgression of the law" (1 John 3:4, KJV). Sin is opposition to the normal mode of existence God intended for us. It is an inversion of reality, rebellion against God's law, and thus it is called "transgression."

In the manifestation of hesed, God is simply continuing to be constant in His identity. Without deviation He is continuing to be who He is toward us even though we have broken trust with Him. Therefore hesed involves the idea of constancy, changelessness, reliability.

"My lovingkindness [hesed] I will not utterly take from him, nor allow My faithfulness to fail. My covenant I will not break, nor alter the word that has gone out of My lips. Once I have sworn by My holiness, I will not lie to David" (Psalm 89:33-35).

The constancy aspect of God's character shows up often in biblical thought:

"If we are faithless, He remains faithful; He cannot deny Himself" (2 Timothy 2:13)—that is, He cannot be untrue to His faithful character even if we are unfaithful.

"Every good gift and every perfect gift is from above, and comes down from the Father of lights, with whom there is no variation or shadow of turning" (James 1:17).

The idea of covenantal love flowing from God to humans was (and is) a revolutionary vision of the divine character. In the setting of the ancient world, it said to the groveling, terrified worshipers of capricious demon gods, "No, that's not God. He is not seeking dominance, nor can He be appeased. Rather, He is a God who gives faithful love and seeks only the same in return."

It was common for humans to think of their gods as requiring loyalty, faithfulness and sacrifice, but here was a God who was pledging Himself to *be* loyal, to *be* faithful, and to *make* sacrifice.

This was new news, and extremely good news for any who would dare to believe it. Abraham did dare to believe it, and God "accounted it to him for righteousness" (Genesis 15:6).

This explains in understandable terms why salvation and righteousness are secured by faith alone, both in the Hebrew Scriptures and the New Testament—because coming into right relation with God is predicated on and motivated by a confident belief that He is a God of a particular character, a God of faithful love.

Any approach to God that is not born of faith is not moved by a true vision of His love and is, therefore, a false approach based on a false conception of His character. If it's not by faith that I come to God, then it's not the one and only true God I'm coming to. If I come to God offering works in exchange for His favor, the basic conception of God's character is wrong, and so I am not actuated by faith in Him as He *is*, but rather by confidence in myself to move Him. I am attempting to relate to God on the premise that my faithfulness

motivates His, rather than on the premise that His faithfulness
motivates mine.

Once hesed is introduced into our vocabulary and understood to be
God's steadfast covenant loyalty, the Old Testament comes alive.
Indeed, the whole Bible starts to make amazing narrative sense. We
come to realize that the writings of Moses and the Prophets collectively
compose a covenant document, a pledge of faithful love, that spells
out in clear historical terms what God's heart looks like in covenant
action and what may be expected from God as He keeps His promise.
The New Testament is seen to be the record of God's covenantal love
having come to full, demonstrable, living form in the person of Jesus
Christ. In the light of hesed, we begin to see God in the most desirable
light imaginable, and the picture is nothing short of revolutionary.

The Ache
I have this friend.

One day we're sitting at a table together. We're eating something. I
am, anyway. He's just picking at his food. Something's wrong.
There's a heaviness about him. I can feel it. He knows I feel it. I
glance up amid the shallow chitchat and catch his eyes in mine for a
steady two seconds. I say with my look, "I know something's wrong,
and I'm here for you."

"Katie's leaving me," he blurts out.

A physical wave of nausea comes over me. His words impact me so
hard I'm immediately sick, and it's not even my experience. It's his
experience, but I feel it through him, and the little I feel compared to
him is so big I can hardly bear it.

My friend is hurting so deep.

So deep I can't comprehend it.

The pain forces tears to his eyes, and to mine.

It's the hurt of being disconnected from the person he gave everything to. And not just disconnected, but rejected. Rejected for someone else.

"I'm just aching inside," he tells me, "because I so want her back."

"I know man. I know you do," is all I can say trying to hold back the tears.

The truth is, there's a hurt that real, but even bigger and more intense, hanging over us all.

Over you.

Over me.

Over the whole world.

It's an ache larger than the universe, because it fills the very heart of infinite God.

Hesed presupposes the divine ache.

Hesed tells us that God feels the disconnect between Himself and us, and He so wants us back.

And hesed tells us that this magnificent God of unfailing love will stop at literally nothing in order to win us back.

That's where we go in the next few chapters.

It's unavoidable.

Because love goes the way of sacrifice.

ten

C O V E N A N T

bram grew up in "Ur of the Chaldeans," a city of Babylonian heritage. This was the "native land" of his family (Genesis 11:27-31). It was a pagan culture steeped in the worship of demons masquerading as deities. "Ur" means *fire*. The city may have been named for a heinous practice common to Babylonian worship. Acting out their distorted picture of God, the people of Babylon performed human sacrifice, in which the victim would be slain on an altar and then burnt to ashes. This was Abram's home.

Joshua records that Abram and his family "dwelt on the other side of the River (the Euphrates) in old times; and they served other gods" (Joshua 24:2). Babylon was Abram's world, his culture and his religion. And with that culture and religion came a particular conception of God that was not true to His character.

But obviously God saw something in this man that made him the prime candidate for forging a new cultural and theological path into a vision of God filled with nearly incomprehensible integrity and moral beauty. So God called the man to "get out" of Babylon, preparatory to getting Babylon completely out of the man. Scripture says, "so Abram departed," revealing the spirit of obedient faith God was looking for.

The Promise
God's goal was not merely to find Abram a nicer place to live. The calling of Abram was the inauguration of a plan that would impact all of human history forward from that point. God says to Abram, "Get out," and then proceeds to make an amazing promise to the whole world to be fulfilled through him:

"I will make you a great nation; I will bless you . . . and you shall be a blessing . . . in you all the families of the earth shall be blessed" (Genesis 12:2-3).

What is here the beginning of a shadowy silhouette to Abram's mind is a crystal clear vision with detailed features in God's mind. This is the second earliest promise-prophecy in the Bible foretelling God's universal embrace of humanity in the coming Messiah (the first is in Genesis 3:15). In Abram's first encounter with this peculiar God, a glorious truth is told: God is committed to all the families of humanity and He is working out a plan to bless the entire world. Abram is the selected genetic and theological vehicle for the plan.

Abram's household grows. He becomes wealthy. His nephew Lot gets in trouble, taken captive by a coalition of kings who attack Sodom. Abram goes on a military rescue mission. He succeeds. Lot is delivered. Abram ends up with "all the goods" (Genesis 14:16) of the defeated army and all that was stolen from Sodom. The king of Sodom thanks Abram for rescuing his people and tells him to keep the goods. Politically nervous and operating on the premise of a higher integrity he is beginning to experience in his relationship with God, Abram declines the offer and returns what belongs to Sodom.

Then comes Abram's second major encounter with the Lord. In the context of Abram returning Sodom's goods, God says, "Do not be afraid, Abram. I am your Shield, your exceedingly great reward" (Genesis 15:1).

The revelation continues to unfold, and it is astounding.

Here is a God who holds Himself in contrast to material wealth as constituting in Himself Abram's "exceeding great reward." The shift here is from what God can give to who God is. He is reward enough in Himself. There is infinite relational value to be found in Him for who He is. To know God and have fellowship with Him is an end, *the* end, in itself. God is guiding Abram to locate significance in other-centered relationship rather than in the self-centered possession of material wealth. A higher motive for existence is being incorporated into Abram's thinking.

Abram gets it. He immediately begins inquiring into God's earlier promise to bless him with offspring and through that offspring to bless the world. He calls the Lord's attention to the fact that he has "no offspring" (Genesis 15:3). God reinforces his promise, assuring Abram that his descendants will rival the number of stars in the night sky and that they will inherit the land of Canaan. Abram says, "Lord, God, how shall I know that I will inherit it?" (Genesis 15:8).

It is at this point that God enters into covenant relation with Abram. He does so by means of a highly significant symbolic ritual (Genesis 15:9-18), which we will consider in detail in a future chapter. For now, we simply need to point out that the covenant was signified by means of a sacrificial ceremony that pointed forward to the One who would someday come through Abram's lineage to bless the whole world. In the ceremonial sacrifice that God instructed Abram to enact, He was answering Abram's question by telling him in symbolism that the covenant will be made good by divine sacrifice. The Lord's very own life will be laid down in love for the world. It is crucial to notice in this second encounter that the promise is dependent on Abram having a son, and on his son having sons, and so on until the One signified by the sacrifice finally arrives.

To The Edge
As the story unfolds, Abram is hyperaware that everything depends

on him and his wife having a son, and he's getting nervous because he and his wife are getting really old.

And everybody knows old people can't have babies.

Abram and Sarai are faced with a biological impossibility.

Which is exactly where God wants them—at the place of the impossible, because ultimately the salvation of humanity is an impossible task that God fully intends to pull off. In His covenantal love, in His hesed, He will follow through. Of course Abram and Sarai don't see it from God's perspective yet. They're still getting to know this new God, and quite literally they have no idea yet what He's capable of, because they don't yet comprehend the enormous power that resides in His love.

But they do know what *they* are capable of, or rather, what they are *not* capable of. And that's where the balance of their dependence resides at present.

So they decide to make it easy on the Lord and get a baby in a way that is, shall we say, really awkward. It was Sarai's idea. If it had been Abram's idea, the awkwardness would have quadzippled. (Yes, I know quadzipple is not a word, but I like it.) Sarai suggests that Abram have a child with her maid, an Egyptian woman named Hagar. The plan worked, and yet it didn't. It worked biologically, but not covenantally.

There was bad theology in the carnal deed; which is to say, the deed revealed a deep-seated misconception of God's character and purpose.

Hagar gets pregnant and feels exalted above Sarai. Sarai gets mad, in both the angry way and the crazy way. The two forms of madness often go together. Abram gets nowhere but in the middle of two women who now hate each other. They name the boy Ishmael. Years pass. Before they know it, the kid is thirteen (and we all know that's scary). Abram and Sarai are shuffling around on walkers and trying to keep track of where they last put their teeth. She's 90 and he's 99.

The Lord has taken them to the edge.

Perfect!

Now some serious revelation can occur.

Divine Potency

At this point they're thinking Ishmael must be what God has in mind, and yet they know he's not what God actually promised. And this is exactly where they need to be for the next phase of the paradigm shift.

"When Abram was ninety-nine years old, the Lord appeared to Abram and said to him, 'I am Almighty God; walk before Me and be blameless. And I will make My covenant between Me and you, and will multiply you exceedingly'" (Genesis 17:1-2).

I hear some emphasis on *Almighty* and on *blameless*. Abraham is clearly out of sync with the covenant. He's gone off manufacturing God's end of the deal, trying to make the impossible stuff come true, trying to fulfill God's promises for Him. And in the process, integrity has been sacrificed. You can hardly blame the guy. He was raised in Babylon, where salvation by human deeds was the prevailing conception of God.

But here comes the Lord of the covenant, undeterred, constant in His faithfulness, making miracles out of messes.

The potency for the fulfillment of the covenant lies in the Lord, not in Abram and Sarai's bodies. So as a not so gentle, but very targeted and effective reminder of human impotence in matters of covenant, the Lord tells Abram that every male in his household and every male henceforth born in his lineage must be circumcised.

Ouch!

Get it?

Abram and all the males in his clan sure did get it, because they did as the Lord commanded. The message was clear: *Not your power, Abram, but Mine is what this covenant will take.* The son born of Abram and Hagar's virility was *not* the promised child.

The Lord is guiding them into a complete reorientation on the landscape of spiritual reality, a reorientation in which the focus is to be locked into Him. All power is to be located in Him. The self-centric obsession that Adam and Eve established in the human psyche is to be completely displaced by the Theo-centric consciousness with which humanity was originally created.

The reversal of the Fall is underway.

That's Funny!

In keeping with the transition of understanding God is taking them through, in an aggressive effort to reconfigure their perception of where the power really lies, at this point in the story God changes their names.

"No longer shall your name be called Abram, but your name shall be Abraham; for *I have* made you a father of many nations. *I will* make you exceedingly fruitful; and *I will* make nations of you, and kings shall come from you. And *I will establish My covenant between Me and you* and your descendants after you in their generations, for an everlasting covenant, to be God to you and your descendants after you" (Genesis 17:5-7).

God's emphasis here is unmistakably clear. The name change signifies that God will accomplish what Abraham cannot. It tells the man, *Shift your focus from yourself to Me.*

As a prophetic hint of her own up-and-coming paradigm shift, the Lord changes Sarai's name as well:

"As for Sarai your wife, you shall not call her name Sarai (*dominative, as in self-assertive*), but Sarah (*princess*) shall be her name. And I will bless her and also give you a son by her" (Genesis 17:15-16).

Amazing!

God tells this precious daughter of His, *You are to cease being self-assertive in relation to my promises. Simply regard yourself as a princess for whom blessing is in store. Expect much from Me.*

Abraham's response to the reiterated promise of a son by Sarah is pretty much what yours and mine would have been:

"Then Abraham fell on his face and laughed, and said in his heart, 'Shall a child be born to a man who is one hundred years old? And shall Sarah, who is ninety years old, bear a child?' And Abraham said to God, 'Oh, that Ishmael might live before You!' Then God said: 'No, Sarah your wife shall bear you a son, and you shall call his name Isaac (*laughter*); I will establish My covenant with him for an everlasting covenant, and with his descendants after him'" (Genesis 17:17-19).

This isn't a chuckle or a giggle. Abraham is on the ground laughing his head off.

A little later Sarah overhears a conversation between the Lord and Abraham in which the Lord says again, "Sarah you wife shall have a son" (Genesis 18:10). Her reflex reaction was the same as Abraham's. More composed than her husband, "Sarah laughed within herself, saying, 'After I have grown old, shall I have pleasure, my lord being old also?'" (Genesis 18:12). She can't imagine engaging in the act by which pregnancy happens, let alone getting pregnant. The whole thing is just hilarious to her.

The ensuing exchange between the Lord and Sarah is theologically rich:

"And the Lord said to Abraham, 'Why did Sarah laugh . . . is anything too hard for the Lord? . . . Sarah shall have a son.' But Sarah denied it, saying, 'I did not laugh,' for she was afraid. And He said, 'No, but you did laugh'" (Genesis 18:13-15).

Of course she did.

It's funny, and we laugh at funny things.

So the Lord flipped the humor on the slow-learning senior citizens by
requiring that they name their son *Funny*, as if to say, *Jokes on you!*
When the promise was fulfilled Abraham bestowed the name God
commanded, no doubt with a new kind of laughter now (Genesis 21:3).
Getting the punch line, Sarah said, "God has made me laugh, so that
all who hear will laugh with me" (Genesis 21:6). The old couple was
now convinced that nothing is "too hard for the Lord!" (Genesis 18:14).

Are you?

Faith Energized By Love
Paul would later explain in his letter to the Galatians that the story
of Abraham and Sarah is an historical metaphor about two very
distinct ways of perceiving our relationship with God, or "two
covenants," one engendering "bondage" and the other granting
"liberty" (Galatians 4:21-26; 5:1).

We can relate to God with the emphasis on ourselves—on a potency
we imagine in ourselves. Or we can relate to God with the emphasis
on Him—on the almighty power of His love to achieve our salvation in
spite of our complete moral bankruptcy. The first is what Paul
portrays as the salvation by works approach (Galatians 2-3). The
second he articulates as a free salvation achieved purely by God's
covenant promise of grace. It's an approach to God that invites us to
embrace His promise by faith, knowing that our faith itself is
empowered by God's love. Paul explains that, "we through the Spirit
eagerly wait for the hope of righteousness by faith. For in Christ Jesus
neither circumcision nor uncircumcision avails anything, but faith
energized by love" (Galatians 5:5-6, literal Greek translation).

In other words, only the power of God's love acting as a new motive
within us can avail to create righteousness in our lives. We come to
know Him as He really is, and in the process of the knowing, His

love awakens in us an enlightened faith, an intelligent trust, based on the truth of our absolute dependence on Him as the One who loves us with absolute faithfulness. And when the things He has promised all along begin to materialize right before our eyes, we will recall that we had previously laughed in unbelief, and then we will laugh with joy.

But that's not the end of the story. The Lord was not done with Abraham yet. His paradigm must shift yet more dramatically, more deeply. In the next chapter we will explore Abraham's most radical encounter with this God of unfailing covenantal love. Abraham is about to gain a vivid mental and emotional picture of God's heart that will forever alter the course of human history and the course of human thought.

Yours and mine included.

I'll be waiting for you in the next chapter.

eleven

C R U C I B L E

*G*aking Abraham to the edge was not enough. The Lord now pushes him over the edge for a really strange and scary freefall. As Abraham is dropping through mid-air, his faith concentrated in the execution of an act commanded by God and yet utterly foreign to His true character, the Lord intervenes to catch His loyal follower in such a way that he lands feet-first with a brilliantly enlightened and purified faith . . .

a faith that can now see the beauty and power of the coming Messiah.

After all the trouble the elderly couple went through to finally get the son of promise, God tells Abraham to do something very odd from our vantage point in covenant history; odd to us, but in keeping with Abraham's cultural and religious upbringing in Babylon:

"Take now your son, your only son Isaac, whom you love, and go to the land of Moriah, and offer him there as a burnt offering" (Genesis 22:2).

Taking into account the various pieces of biblical information regarding Abraham's story, along with the historical setting Scripture portrays, I'd like to suggest that a convergence of three things is happening here:

1. God is testing Abraham's faith. Does he now understand that God is faithful to fulfill His promises, that human impotence is no hindrance for the Lord, and that only a lack of obedient faith can interfere?

2. God is cleansing Abraham's faith from every lingering trace of the appeasement or salvation-by-works theology with which he was raised in Babylon, initiating a theological lineage of enlightened faith free from the pagan idea that God demands suffering in exchange for His favor.

3. God is creating in Abraham a sense of the mental and emotional anguish He Himself will endure on a much larger scale of intensity in the giving of His only Son for the salvation of the world.

Severe Object Lesson

From our place in history we can't help but wonder, *What in the world was God thinking when He told Abraham to make his son Isaac a human sacrifice?* The same God later told Moses that this practice was an "abomination" in His sight and one of the reasons it was necessary that the Canaanites and their demon gods be defeated (Deuteronomy 12:29-31). If any post-Moses follower of Yahweh were to hear a voice requiring human sacrifice, the voice would be regarded as that of any god but the true One. Then why would God command Abraham, His faithful follower, to lay his child on an altar, slit the boy's throat, and burn him to ashes? We find the story difficult to swallow.

Ah, but this strange biblical drama, so out of character for a God who abhors human sacrifice, begins to make sense in Abraham's historical and spiritual context, if not in that of Moses or ourselves. Making Abraham walk such a daunting spiritual gauntlet could only possess rationale if the possibility of God requiring human sacrifice was an existing fear lurking in Abraham's time and culture. And watching God intervene at the last moment to stop Abraham from doing the very thing He had commanded him to do, only makes sense if God was actually attempting to shift Abraham's focus to another sacrifice, a sacrifice that the man himself could not ultimately make. Of course, those who have read the story after the fact know that God was doing just that. He was bringing Christ to view as the coming sacrifice for mankind.

We are stunned by the fact that Abraham proceeded to carry out the sacrifice of Isaac, and would have completed the grim task if God had not stopped him. This reveals that Abraham already held, to some degree, ideas from his upbringing that would at least allow for human sacrifice, although, knowing God as He did, the command must have been perplexing.

We have good reason to believe that the pagan culture in which Abraham was raised did practice human sacrifice, reflective of a grossly distorted perception of the divine identity. Before he received the call of God, Abraham lived in a popular Babylonian city called "Ur of the Chaldeans" (Genesis 11:28). The biblical record informs us that Abraham was raised in a home that "served other gods" (Joshua 24:2). This is a fact that is rarely taken into account when Abraham's story is assessed. Scripture also tells us that those "other gods" were none other than "demons" masquerading as deities. These demon "gods" required human sacrifice and in so doing misrepresented the character of the one and only true God (Psalm 106:36-38). This is Abraham's background, which is helpful to know as we try to make sense of this singular biblical account of God commanding a human sacrifice.

We must remember that while Abraham faithfully responded to the call of the true God to leave Babylon, he was the man with whom the monotheistic Hebrew faith was *begun*. As such, he had much to learn, as is made evident by his Hagar and Ishmael escapade. When he heard the voice of God telling him to depart from his home and venture into a whole new land, he was being led into a whole new belief system as well. Abraham was called out of Babylon, and now the Lord needed to get Babylon completely out of Abraham. Before this honest man could become the father of a new and true theological lineage, He needed to understand that there was a marked distinction between the false theology common to the religion of his ancestors and the truth about God.

In this historic context is easy to see that God subjected Abraham to such a trying experience, not because God is actually of such a character to demand human sacrifice, but rather to test Abraham's faith, to purify his faith, and to reveal God's own heart of self-sacrificing love.

First, Abraham must demonstrate his devotion to God by manifesting an unswerving obedience in the context of the knowledge he had.

Next, he must accept a massive paradigm shift from a god who requires sacrifice to a God who makes sacrifice.

And finally, in the process, he must feel to the depths of his soul the pain God would have to endure to save the human race.

Abraham's experience was the embryonic beginnings of an obedience, of a faith, and of a theology that would reach its zenith of glory at the cross of Christ.

Divine Iconoclast

In commanding Abraham to sacrifice Isaac, we are witnessing the divine genius in iconoclastic motion. (The word *iconoclast* simply refers to one who crushes false images of God, an idol smasher.) God was on a mission to destroy the false image of Himself so prevalent in Abraham's day (and in our own day as well, though in the more subtle form of merit-based approaches to salvation) in order to replace it with the true knowledge of His character. This Yahweh God, who had newly introduced Himself to Abraham as distinct from the gods of his upbringing in the Babylonian worship cult, was on a quest to extract from Abraham's thinking, and from the thinking of all who would follow his lead, every vestige of the salvation by works theology with which he had been educated.

It was precisely because God so deeply detests human sacrifice and the idea that His favor can be earned, and because He so desperately

longs to be known as the unappeasable God of love He really is, that
He told Abraham to sacrifice Isaac only to stay his trembling hand at
the last minute. It was the Lord's plan all along to stop Abraham in
his theological tracks as the blade was moving through the air
toward Isaac. The experience God led Abraham through was an
emancipation exercise, a spiritual odyssey devised to uproot from
Abraham's thinking the idea that God is a deity whose anger can be
satiated by suffering and whose saving action can be merited. It was
a theological and emotional journey of radical liberation. One image
needed to be destroyed and another put in its place.

Abraham's obedience to God's command revealed that while his faith
was in need of further enlightenment, he was, nonetheless, honest in
his faith and determined to follow Yahweh wherever He might lead. This
spirit of devotion made it possible for God to grow Abraham's faith.

The same holds true for all of us. God will develop the faith of every
person who is honestly devoted to whatever they know of Him, be it
little or much. Obedience to God, even when mingled with erroneous
ideas of who God is and what He requires, constitutes a posture of
mind and heart that makes it possible for God, the great Iconoclast,
to gradually crush every false theological image we hold and
progressively set us free with deeper and yet deeper liberty. Only
those who are honestly committed to what they believe are
psychologically prepared to learn more and to have their belief
system cleansed. Abraham was such a man.

The Test
The Bible says God told Abraham to sacrifice his son to "test" him.
Such a test would make no sense if Abraham had clearly understood
that human sacrifice is an abomination to the Lord and an unthinkable
evil, as later prophets believed. If Abraham were completely clear on the
matter and had not been raised in Babylon, the test would have been
equivalent to God asking the man to commit an evil act in violation of
his conscience simply to see if he would do it.

So in what sense did God's command to Abraham constitute a test? It was a test of obedient faith. Abraham must obey the voice of God and thus reveal God's heart. Abraham needed to demonstrate that He had total confidence in God to devise another plan if Isaac were sacrificed. Hebrews 11:17-19 tells us that Abraham did have such faith, and the test revealed his faith. He believed God could raise Isaac from the dead if need be. With a spirit of determined obedience he proceeded to offer up his son to God who, at the last minute, proved that He actually requires no such sacrifice. "Do not lay your hand on the lad," God said, "or do anything to him; for now I know that you fear God, since you have not withheld your son, your only *son*, from Me" (Genesis 22:12). At the same time, in the process of the test, Abraham would experience a taste of God's future anguish in giving His Son for the salvation of humanity. Two pictures would be presented to him, the first in keeping with the theology popular in his culture, the second radically different and prophetic of the coming Messiah.

God was leading His faithful friend through a painful but necessary paradigm shift, while making him a medium of revelation. Abraham was asked to walk an extremely difficult but effective educational path for all future generations. He was called upon to break new theological ground. Master psychologist that He is, God required of Abraham what the guilty and deceived human heart inclines us all to believe God might ultimately require of us. Then, at Abraham's most committed point, God intervened. He shattered the ugly image and constructed within Abraham's heart an entirely new image—of a God who would Himself suffer and die for human redemption.

God Will Provide The Sacrifice

By telling Abraham to sacrifice Isaac, God seemingly confirmed what Abraham feared might be true. (See Matthew 15:21-28, where Jesus used the same method to teach His disciples that their perception of His character was wrong.) But He only did so as a teaching device in order to confirm Abraham's obedience and to forge a new pattern of thinking in his mind. By means of this most severe test, God aroused in Abraham an acute emotional sense of the false image that haunts us all as a legacy from the Fall. Then, at the peak point of horrific clarity, God crushed the image out of existence and introduced a whole new spiritual realization. When the frightful shadow loomed over Abraham's head in its darkest hue, just as he was about to drive the knife into his son, God broke the dark spell that must be broken in all of our hearts. As the blade was lifted over his child, tears flowing and body trembling, God stepped in to stay the old man's hand. What joyous relief must have flooded Abraham's heart when he "lifted his eyes and looked, and there behind him was a ram caught in a thicket by its horns" (Genesis 22:13).

The message came through loud and clear:

"No, Abraham! That's not how it works. That's not *Me*, my faithful friend. Your willingness to make this sacrifice reveals that you trust Me, but no such sacrifice is needed. Now, since you trust Me so confidently, listen carefully to what I'm about to tell you: I will provide the sacrifice to save you and all your children! You can't make the sacrifice needed to save your soul, and I do not require you to. I will make the sacrifice. *I* will, not you. The sacrifice for your salvation is Mine alone to make by virtue of My love for you."

In that cathartic moment of bright epiphany, Abraham underwent a kind of spiritual shock treatment that jolted him into the beautiful realization that God, so far from being an appeasable deity whose favor must be earned, is a God of infinite love who has pledged Himself to undergo the only sacrifice necessary to save fallen humanity. As Abraham lifted the knife over Isaac, he tasted, ever so slightly by comparison, the pain that God alone would endure in giving His only Son for the salvation of this lost world so lost to love.

And so, basking in the light of God's extravagant grace, anticipating the coming Savior, "Abraham called the name of the place, The-LORD-Will-Provide" (Genesis 22:14).

Yes He will, and He has.

But only at great personal loss.

twelve

S U N D E R I N G

bove, beyond, and before all things is an infinite intimacy.

And we're invited in.

We live in a universe defined by and designed for covenant, which is a biblical way of saying we live in a universe created by a God of relational faithfulness. Covenant is an idea that simply means there is more than one person and that those who coexist live toward one another with other-centered integrity.

The most ancient of all covenantal relationships is the one that has always existed between God the Father, God the Son, and God the Holy Spirit.

The Father calls the Son, "the Man who is My Companion" and the "One in whom My Soul delights" (Zechariah 13:7; Isaiah 42:1). The pre-incarnate Son articulates the relationship between Himself and the Father as involving "daily . . . delight" and "enjoying" one another's "company" (Proverbs 8:30-31, NKJV and Msg). Jesus reminisces to the Father about their relationship in eternity past with the tender prayer, "You loved Me before the foundation of the world" (John 17:24). The Holy Spirit is said to be a personal being who engages in comfort, communication, and communion (John 16:7-13; 2 Corinthians 13:14). And John tells us that "these three are One" (1 John 5:7), indicating their intimate fellowship with one another. God has always known desire and its perfect satisfaction. At the core of the essential divine identity is an unbroken faithfulness of infinite proportions and magnificent beauty.

Covenant Of Creation

Then, from the matrix of God's eternal other-centered love, another covenant was formed: the covenant of creation. Within the triune divine fellowship an agreement was made:

"Let Us make man in Our image, according to Our likeness" (Genesis 1:26).

Beings bearing the divine likeness, with the capacity to conceive, feel, and choose love were to be brought into existence. The self-giving love of God was to be replicated.

What an excellent plan!

Father, Son and Spirit ventured into the covenant of Creation knowing full well what they were doing. They were perfectly aware of the risk involved in creating beings adjacent to themselves who would be genuinely autonomous sharers in the wonder of existence.

The risk is obvious: to the possibility of love is the possibility of anti-love and all the horrors it entails.

But God deemed the sure future of an infinitely expanding love worth the sure pain to get there.

You can argue with Him about it if your own pain has been more than you can bear. You may be tempted, as I have been at times, to think it would have been better if you had never existed, but He still loves you and He's so very glad you do exist. He knows your pain, and He knows it with teary eyes and aching heart. *His* pain includes yours and everyone else's on top of His own. But knowing the pain, He also knew the potential. So He ventured forward. The covenant of Creation was made.

And so, here we are, you and I.

But watch now as the story becomes more beautiful still.

Covenant Of Peace

Immediately joined to the covenant of creation was the covenant of peace.

"'The mountains shall depart and the hills be removed, but My kindness [hesed] shall not depart from you, nor shall My covenant of peace be removed,' says the Lord, who has mercy on you" (Isaiah 54:10).

"For I know the thoughts that I think toward you, says the Lord, thoughts of peace and not of evil, to give you a future and a hope" (Jeremiah 29:11).

Father, Son and Holy Spirit knew they would love us more than themselves the moment we would be brought into existence. Such is the nature of love. Self is always secondary to others. They also knew in advance of our rebellion. And so they entered into a sacred corporate oath to save humanity at any and all cost to themselves. This is the covenant of peace. This is God continuing to be who God is—a God of relational integrity and faithfulness.

To fulfill the covenant of peace, an infinitely painful fracture of the divine fellowship would be necessary. Within the Trinity, it was agreed that the Son would become the incarnate One. Jesus was to be given to the fallen human race as the embodiment of the covenant. Therefore, He was named "the Prince of the Covenant"

(Daniel 11:22) and was sent into our world to "confirm the covenant" by His self-sacrificing death (Daniel 9:26-27).

In tender, supportive words the Father spoke to the Son before the incarnation:

"I, the LORD, have called You in righteousness, and will hold Your hand; I will keep You and give You as a covenant to the people" (Isaiah 42:6).

The Father here promises to hold the Son's hand through the journey, indicating that it will be a difficult ordeal, and also indicating that God is the kind of being who holds hands, which is just absolutely brilliant (as in, illuminating) if you think about it.

This prophecy states that Jesus would be given to the world as God's covenant.

He *is* the covenant.

In total.

He is the whole package of covenantal love acted out from both sides—the divine side and the human side. He was relationally faithful as *God to humanity*, and He was relationally faithful as *man to God*. Faith was kept in Christ, whole and complete.

But how exactly did Jesus constitute the covenant?

How did He keep faith?

In ancient times, it was understood that a covenant involved the total commitment of the covenant makers to one another. To signify this commitment, an animal sacrifice was severed in two, and laid out on the ground with each half across from the other forming a path between them. Then each party engaging in the covenant would walk between the pieces, thus signifying that each one was giving themselves to the other, cutting themselves in half, as it were, in the giving action. No stronger form of commitment was conceivable. To enter into covenant was equivalent to giving one's self away. It is not surprising, then, that the word "covenant" is *beriyth* in Hebrew and literally means to *cut off* or *cut in two*.

It was in this cultural context that God entered into covenant with Abraham:

"So He said to him, 'Bring Me a three-year-old heifer, a three-year-old female goat, a three-year-old ram, a turtledove, and a young pigeon.' Then he brought all these to Him and cut them in two, down the middle, and placed each piece opposite the other; but he did not cut the birds in two. And when the vultures came down on the carcasses, Abram drove them away. Now when the sun was going down, a deep sleep fell upon Abram; and behold, horror *and* great darkness fell upon him. . . . And it came to pass, when the sun went down and it was dark, that behold, there appeared a smoking oven and a burning torch that passed between those pieces. On the same day the LORD made a covenant with Abram" (Genesis 15:9-12, 17-18).

This is the earliest biblical prophecy regarding the sacrifice God would make in order to remain faithful to the covenant of peace. Here was revealed to Abraham the horrific suffering the triune God would voluntarily endure in order to save fallen humanity. When the reality of this symbolism played out, it involved a severing of the Godhead, or as one peculiarly insightful author has articulated the ordeal, "the "sundering of the divine Powers," referring to the Father, Son, and Holy Spirit (E.G. White, *Bible Commentary*, vol. 7, p. 924).

Only that which is one can be sundered.

Only that which is cohesive can be severed.

And so, we cannot contemplate the sacrifice of Christ without being reminded that He didn't come into our world out of nowhere. His birth as a human being was not His beginning. He hails from a deep place of mind-boggling relational love in eternity past. John opens

His gospel by informing us that Jesus came into our world from "the bosom of the Father" (John 1:18). Another Bible translation renders the text less poetic and more direct: Jesus is the One "who lives in the closest intimacy with the Father" (Phi). This God who holds hands is also a God who shares His bosom. His inmost heart is a place of close companionship.

And that's where Jesus came from,

where He was "cut off" from,

to become the covenant pledge of God's unfailing love for wayward humanity.

He said of His origin, "I came forth from the Father and have come into the world" (John 16:28). For eternal ages past, from the far reaches of the infinite before, Jesus had always lived with the Father and the Holy Sprit in joyous, self-giving love. They were a social unit of unimaginable bliss until the moment of His condescension into Mary's womb.

Then everything changed.

Then He was voluntarily severed from the fellowship.

For Christ, the covenant of peace entailed His departure from the bosom of the divine intimacy. And the remaining members of the Godhead suffered the severing, as well. The Father was heard by the inhabited universe to cry out, "Awake, O sword, against My Shepherd, against the Man who is My Companion" (Zechariah 13:7).

The covenant is painful for God, and yet freely chosen.

In the language of the covenant, harkening back to the ceremony in which Abraham cut the animal sacrifices in half, the prophet Daniel foretold, "Messiah shall be cut off, but not for Himself," and "He shall confirm a covenant" (Daniel 9:26-27).

And why did He do all this?

For love of you and me.

For love of your kid's soccer coach and the lady you paid for your groceries today.

For love of the no-name face in Afghanistan you recently saw on the news.

Cutting Deep Into God

The cutting off process first involved the incarnation and then led to the cross.

Paul says that Jesus, "being in very nature God, did not consider equality with God something to be grasped, but made Himself nothing" (Philippians 2:6-7 NIV). The Greek word here translated, "nothing," is *kenosis*. "Nothing" is a good translation. Another version captures the meaning of *kenosis* with the word "emptied." He "emptied Himself" (NASB).

But emptied Himself of what, exactly?

Getting more specific to what it would mean for God to empty Himself, yet another Bible translation says, He "did not cling to His privileges as God's equal, but stripped Himself of every advantage" (Phi).

Now we're getting to the heart of the divine self-emptying.

There are specific "advantages"—we might call them *powers* or *abilities*—that pertain to God alone and to no created beings: omnipotence, omniscience, and omnipresence.

It is these that Christ emptied from Himself when He became human.

When Scripture says of Christ, "The Child grew and became strong in spirit, filled with wisdom" (Luke 2:40), it is describing a real developmental growth in both strength and knowledge. When Jesus plainly stated that He did not *know* the "day and hour" of His second coming, but that the Father does know, He was indicating that His personal omniscience was not operable during His time on earth (Mark 10:32). And when Christ said, "I can of Myself do nothing" (John 5:30), looking to the Father for power as any human must, He made clear that His personal omnipotence was made inoperable, as well. Christ did not enter our world with His innate divine abilities intact, but rather laid them aside. "For He, who has always been God by nature, did not cling to His privileges as God's equal, but stripped Himself of every advantage by consenting to . . . be born a man" (Philippians 2:6-7, Phi).

The incarnation was not an appearance of condescension, but an actual transmigration of nature for God. A literal alteration of the divine reality was entailed in the severing. God the Son truly became human in the person of Jesus Christ. "Since the children have flesh and blood, He too shared in their humanity . . . made like His brothers in every way" (Hebrews 2:14, 17, NIV). Therefore, His experience in our flesh was totally authentic. It involved becoming, as it were, "nothing" by comparison to what He had previously been. He never ceased to be fully divine, but in an astounding act of self-sacrificing love He literally became human and in so doing He voluntarily put His divine powers in remission.

But why was such a radical move necessary for God?

The incarnation was necessary, Paul explains, so that Christ "might taste death for everyone" (Hebrews 2:9). The death Paul has in mind here is that death which constitutes the final and full "wages of sin" (Romans 6:23), which involves the soul bearing the horrific reality of its guilt and being plunged into eternal separation from God (Romans 2:1-9; Revelation 20:11-15). We can easily imagine that if Christ had come to our world and gone to the cross with His divine powers operable, the desperate cry, "My God, My God, why have You forsaken Me?" would have meant nothing, for the simple reason that, all the while, He would have been transcending the event by means of His omniscience and omnipresence. The most we could say of the cross would be that it was a very convincing act, but not a real psychological experience for Him. But by becoming truly human, Christ did, in fact, submit Himself to the necessary set of conditions that would make it possible for Him to genuinely experience all the dark horror of our corporate guilt. In so doing, He underwent the complete separation from God that our sin imposes. As He faced the bleak mental and emotional reality of that death without manifesting any impulse to abandon us to save Himself, we find ourselves face to face with the fact that God literally loves us more than His own life. In Christ, the selfless nature of God's love was authentically *demonstrated* for us, "in that while we were still sinners, Christ died for us" (Romans 5:8). In the epic act of self-emptying entailed in the incarnation and the cross, God has forever defined Himself in our eyes. And the revelation is breathtaking.

The Nature Of Sin And Guilt

Someone will ask, "But why did Jesus have to die for our salvation? How is the God of the Bible any different than the ancient pagan gods that required human sacrifice for their appeasement? If God is love, why couldn't He just forgive us out of the sheer goodness of His heart without Jesus having to suffer and die?"

Well, the short answer is, that's exactly what the cross does reveal—God forgiving us out of the sheer goodness of His heart! But that goodness came at a price to Him due to the very nature of sin and of forgiveness.

Once we understand the incarnation, we realize that the One hanging on the cross is none other than God Himself. Therefore, we witness no appeasement sacrifice at the cross of Christ. Actually, what we see at the cross is God maintaining the very love by which appeasement cannot be made to Him. The cross was God's own sacrifice for us, not anyone else's sacrifice to God. Rather than channel His justifiable anger toward us and demand that we pay for our sins, God chose rather to bear the loss in Himself, to take the hit our sin dealt to Him and refuse to return the hit to us.

Our salvation could not be achieved without the suffering of Christ because suffering is innate to sin, and because suffering is innate to the forgiveness of sin.

Every time a sin is committed there is suffering. The victim suffers loss to some degree on some level—material loss, mental loss, emotional loss, social loss, or loss in all these areas. Those who know and love the victim suffer loss, as well. Also, the perpetrator of any given sin suffers loss in moral worth and in his capacity for love. And by virtue of His love for each one, God suffers more than all those involved. Plain and simple, sin imposes injury. It is never a pain-free matter. Every wrongdoing carries an inherent cost because sin is real violation. It is not an arbitrarily designated category. Sin always involves actual violation of the integrity of a relationship.

Then, once committed, sin becomes an existing reality in the mind in the form of guilt. While God does hate and condemn our sin, the guilt of sin is not conjured up by God and artificially imposed upon us. Sin is not only a legal problem, it's an experiential problem—a problem that resides in the very character and conscience of the sinner. In fact, God's legal system is the only one that actually, truly, and accurately represents the reality of relational experience.

Sin is defined in Scripture as "transgression of the law" (1 John 3:4, KJV). The law of God is not merely an arbitrarily concocted and externally imposed list of behavioral rules. All of the behaviors prescribed in God's law are behaviors that constitute other-centered love, and all of the behaviors forbidden in God's law constitute violations of the relational integrity love requires. The law is love and sin is anti-love.

This is why the Ten Commandment law of God is called, "the covenant" (Exodus 34:28). Covenant means relational faithfulness, or other-centered love. The Ten Commandments spell out what covenantal love looks like in action.

Sin, or "transgression of the Law," is the failure to love God and others. And because God's law of love is innate to God's very character and, therefore, innate to the way God made us to operate as creatures of covenant, sin is more than a legal problem. It's a relational problem. The problem reaches down into our very identities. The problem is actually in us.

Paul says:

"The law is holy, and the Commandment holy and just and good . . . but I am carnal, sold under sin . . . For I know that in me (that is, in my flesh) nothing good dwells" (Romans 7:12, 14, 18).

Jeremiah says:

"Sin . . . is written with a pen of iron; with the point of a diamond it is engraved on the tablet of their heart" (Jeremiah 17:1).

Every relational violation impacts the mind of the transgressor in at least two real ways: (1) The inclination of the character is bent a little more toward selfishness and (2) guilt comes upon the conscience. Even if we attempt to rationalize our violations, guilt is still present beneath all our surface excuses. Shame resides in the soul and manifests itself in various ways:

• Defensiveness.

• Noticing and commenting upon the failures and weaknesses of others.

• An inflated ego, projecting one's self as better than others or making sure people are aware of your achievements.

• Addiction to or obsession with anything: food, TV, sex, drugs, flirtatiousness, fame, attention, success, work, danger.

• False narratives, portraying one's life to be something it's not.

All of these behaviors are evasion maneuvers and coping mechanisms we employ in an attempt to deal with the internal reservoir of guilt that sin stores up in the conscience.

Sin is an actual "thing" of moral, psychological, and emotional weight. We carry it inside of us. Paul says we become "loaded down with sin" (2 Timothy 3:6). Jesus says we are "heavy laden" (Matthew 11:28). Sin is born within us in the form of guilt. The Bible speaks of the fact that we all have "an evil conscience" (Hebrews 10:22). If we think of sin as merely breaking imposed rules that have no bearing on our actual moral condition, we fail to grasp what sin is. God's law is grounded in the reality of God's character. It is not a random list of prohibitions intended to be a means of exercising authority over us to show us He's boss. Rather, it defines what faithful love looks like and forbids everything that affects relational ruin.

"God is love," by which Scripture means to convey that God is completely self-giving and other-centered in all His thoughts, feelings, and actions. Said another way, God is relationally faithful to all others above and before Himself. This God created humanity in His image, meaning God designed us mentally, emotionally, and biologically to live with one another in self-giving love. Sin is contrary to this design, and is therefore manifested in every form of relational violation. It is not surprising then that Paul defines sin and sinners with numerous relational terms:

Maliciousness, envy, murder, strife, deceit, backbiting, haters of God, violence, inventors of evil things, disobedient to parents, untrustworthy, covenant-breakers, unforgiving (Romans 1:29-31), self seeking (Romans 2:8), unmerciful, lovers of self, lovers of money, unthankful, unloving, slanderers, brutal, traitors, lovers of pleasure rather than lovers of God (2 Timothy 3:1-4).

Please notice that everything Paul names as sin involves individuals breaking trust with one another. Sin always involves crossing the line of freedom to cause hurt, which means that sin always involves violating the principle of love.

Since this is the nature of sin, it is evident that the guilt of sin is actual, not artificial; intrinsic, not extrinsic. Sin is a psychological reality carried in the soul in the form of shame, self-loathing, and a sense of condemnation. Even when we evade our guilt by various suppression techniques, it's still there inside of us as a secret horror that will be brought to the surface of the conscience at some point.

A Debt To Be Paid

We can understand, then, that here is a sense in which sin creates a debt or a penalty that must be paid (Matthew 18:21-35; 2 Peter 2:1; 1 Corinthian 6:20; 7:23). This economic terminology calls our attention to the sublime reality that sin is a *taking* action. It uses up the value and energies of others without giving in return. It violates others and in so doing it creates a moral deficit. Sin costs something. It drains relational, emotional, mental, and even physical resources. It creates a real imbalance in the flow of reciprocal love. As a result, *debt* is acquired. Sin breaks covenant. God has loved us, but we have not loved Him. There is a failure on our part to give Him love in response to His love. We owe Him for all that we have failed to give Him and for all the hurt we have inflicted on Him. The same is true of all our interhuman relations as well. In the process of violating one another, we have failed to be true, good, and giving. As a result, our world is filled with relational discrepancies and debts of love.

Now all this moral debt does not simply vanish after accruing. It literally exists in the mental realm of those who have committed the sins. It exists in the form of shame, broken relationships, damaged minds and injured hearts. There is a heavy sense that we all carry in us that something is dreadfully wrong with each of us individually and with our world as a whole. It hovers just beneath the surface of our consciousness, palpable at any given moment to the degree that we don't evade it, numb it, medicate it, or offload it by means of blame-casting or delusions of self-righteousness. Guilt is just there, or rather *here*, in us as individuals and as a world.

So the question becomes, What is God to do with our guilt? How is the debt to be disposed of? By what means may it be liquidated?

How is the inequity to be brought to balance?

There are only two possible solutions: God can either require us to pay up by demanding that we undo all our wrongs and from this day forward live in perfect love for God and all others, or God can forgive us and by the power of forgiveness restore us to love. In the first instance, it is evident that we cannot pay our debt short of paying with our very lives, and even then the damage done by our wrongs would not be righted. If God did not love us, He could simply destroy us in an instant and be done with the whole painful ordeal. But He does love us. So, He chooses to forgive us rather than zap us out of existence. But here's the thing about forgiveness: it is costly and painful. By choosing to forgive, God has chosen to endure the suffering forgiveness requires.

Any time a person chooses to forgive a wrong, they are in effect choosing to bear whatever loss, injury, or violation was imposed upon them. A distinct dying to self is involved. This was one aspect of the suffering we see Christ enduring on the cross. By bearing our sin against Him without retaliating, He accepted the suffering inherent to forgiveness, the suffering required in order to release us from the moral debt we owe. He spoke His heart in the words, "Father, forgive them, for they do not know what they do" (Luke 23:34). As Jesus hung there upon the cross, He suffered only to the degree that He kept on forgiving us instead of dealing out to us the punishment we actually deserved. The measure of His suffering was the measure of His love, facing off against the measure of our guilt.

He bore our sin.

He carried it.

He absorbed it in Himself.

He endured all our hate and selfishness by refusing to reflect it back to us, and in so doing He exhausted its power to destroy. He was victorious over our sin by never participating in it and by loving us beyond it. To all of the hostility that flows out of humanity toward one another and toward Him, He says,

It stops here!

This dies with me!

No more hate!

No more sin!

No more shame!

Let forgiveness reign!

The Sinbearer

And yet, there was something more that happened at the cross.

Jesus also experientially bore our sin and its guilt in His own person.

In Scripture, the word *experience* does not occur. The concept is present, however, in the Hebrew words, *yada* (know) and *deeth* (knowledge), which refer to experiential intimacy, close personal identification, oneness. It is in this sense that the Father says of His Son's entrance into our world, "By His knowledge [*deeth*] My righteous Servant shall justify many, for He shall bear their iniquities" (Isaiah 53:11).

Jesus became the Savior of the world by *knowledge* and by *bearing*. There is some real sense in which He *knew* us and *bore* our iniquities. He did not bear our sins as some sort of physical weight, obviously, nor even as a mere legal penalty. The truth of the matter is much deeper than that and far more horrific.

But there is beauty beyond the horror.

Jesus became our Sinbearer in the most concrete and literal sense. He experienced the reality of our guilt as though it were His own.

When Christ hung on the cross, the mental and emotional weight of the sin of the world came upon Him in full force. In the words of Isaiah, "The Lord has laid on Him the iniquity of us all. . . . His soul [was made] an offering for sin. . . . He poured out His soul unto death, and He was numbered with the transgressors, and bore the sin of many" (Isaiah 53:6, 10, 12).

By virtue of the incarnation Christ, the Father's eternal divine Son entered into complete solidarity with the fallen human race. An intimate bond of experiential oneness was formed in Jesus between divinity and humanity. By means of genuine identification and sympathetic union, Jesus enveloped in Himself the psychological reality of our sin and shame. Love by its very nature identifies with the suffering of others. Love feels. By love Christ entered the dark region of human guilt and faced it in all its unbuffered force.

The cutting off process that began with the incarnation unfolded upon Christ with increased force as He entered the garden of Gethsemane, and then reached its zenith of intensity as He hung upon the cross.

Having taken our human nature upon Himself with all its limitations, Jesus now became the Sinbearer for fallen humanity. Expressing the internal nature of His sacrificial agony, Jesus told His disciples as they entered the garden, "My soul [*psyche* in the Greek] is exceedingly sorrowful, even to death" (Matthew 26:38).

The cutting is reaching deep into Him. The sacrificial "pieces" are now severed and laid out on the ground opposite one another. The path of suffering and sacrifice is marked out. It is a "soul" sacrifice He is making, a sacrifice of His total being.

From the garden He went to the cross. Peter says that Jesus "Himself bore our sins in His own body on the tree" (1 Peter 2:24). Paul goes so far as to say, "For He [the Father] made Him [Jesus] who knew no sin to be sin for us, that we might become the righteousness of God in Him" (2 Corinthians 5:21). This is the Bible's way of telling us that Jesus took into His heart and mind the total reality of our sin and shame. The result was complete separation from the Father. As He hung upon the cross, Jesus cried out, "My God, My God, why have You forsaken Me?" (Matthew 27:46).

Now the severing was final and complete. He felt to the depths of His being the massive chasm of separation that sin makes between God and man. He felt the full weight of the broken covenant on man's side even as He maintained covenant honor from God's side. He bore the guilt entailed in our lack of love while proving the faithfulness of God by continuing to love us "to the end" (John 13:1).

With His expiring breath, "It is finished" (John 19:30), the truth about God was known with crystal clarity.

At the cross we witness God's hierarchy of value, and to our utter astonishment He places higher value on us than on Himself. We see in Christ God's disposition toward Himself in relation to us, and it is this: He would literally rather cease to exist than to let us perish in our sins.

And this means that we are in the very best of all situations imaginable!

We are loved with a perfectly selfless love that may be trusted with perfect trust. In God's love there is an immovable stability in which we can forever rest, beginning this very moment. His love holds before us the potential for an eternally sustainable relational bliss. We are safe, after all. We are secure. We are contained, not in an ultimately scary and unpredictable universe, but rather in an ultimately friendly universe created by an ultimately friendly God . . .

a God who holds hands and opens His bosom for fellowship,

a God of unswerving faithfulness,

a God who was torn asunder and cut to the depths of His being for love of you and me.

thirteen

U N I L A T E R A L

*I*f there is one word that means more than any other, and yet has been slaughtered nearly beyond recognition, that word is love. It's the most over-used and misunderstood word going.

I love surfing.

I love tacos.

I love my wife.

But I'm feeling like there should be some significant difference between my wife and tacos.

On any given day, within any given hour, you can turn on the radio and hear about love over and over again.

Or maybe not.

I once heard that a popular music magazine did a word search in their huge database of lyrics. They wanted to discover the most frequently used words in pop music. Not surprisingly, the word *love* was number one. The second most frequently used word turned out to be *baby*, not as a synonym for infant, of course, but as in, "Baby, I love you because you're such a beautiful babe." The third most frequently used word in pop music is *yeah*, as in, "Baby, I love you, oh yeah!" There's even a band by the name, *The Yeah, Yeah, Yeahs.*

Love is the theme of just about every pop album, and yet one has to wonder, "What's love got to do with it?" (Tina Turner). The lyrical content usually follows a familiar pattern.

Track one: Oh baby, I love you, oh, oh, oh, yeah, yeah, yeah.

Track two: Oh no baby, I don't love you anymore, yeah, yeah, yeah. Breaking up is hard to do, baby, oh yeah, but a more babeable babe has come along, so adios.

Track three: Baby (not the same baby mentioned on previous tracks), I'm so in love with you, and you're the only one for me, yeah, yeah, yeah, until track four, of course.

I might be exaggerating a little, but you get the point. There's always some more babeable babe to love, *oh yeah.*

But here's the thing about love as popularly conceived:

It's not.

Not in the sense that God is love, at least.

Pop Love
When I "love" you because of what you do for me, love isn't actually occurring from my side of the relationship, because "love" that is focused inward is really selfishness. It's not you I love, baby, it's me.

And that's why, when somebody comes along that I think is better for me, you're dispensable.

It's like the woman who said to me in a marriage counseling session, "My husband doesn't love me. He uses me to love himself. I'm like a tool in his shed."

Human love is severely broken.

So we talk of love and sing of love obsessively, and yet we are in a continual crisis of love. We know, in our honest moments, that our natural bent is toward self-centeredness and we know that it leaves us empty. But somewhere in our hearts we also sense that there is another kind of love, of a whole different quality, that we might experience if only we could *find* the right person or *be* the right person. So we keep hoping and trying and failing and still hoping and trying again.

Pop love—one pop artist scorns it as "designer love" (The Goo Goo Dolls, *Better Days*)—is initiated when an individual notices something in another person that promises pleasure. The attraction is outward, but with an inward motivation. The unspoken sensation is, "I see something in you of potential benefit to me." The *other* is seen only with reference to *self.*

This is what the ancient Greeks called eros.

You know eros well because the popular culture of ancient Greece was no different than our pop culture of today. Eros, by any other name, is the prevailing love of every pop culture in every era of history, because eros, at least in its broken form, is nothing more or less than the corporate expression of the fallen human condition. It is the societal outworking of each person's impulse to compete for self-gratification, exploiting everything and everybody of value. Self is the center of reality, and each item and entity is perceived as having value only to the degree that it has potential to satisfy self-centered desires.

In Greek mythology, Eros was the god of sexual love, the son of Aphrodite. In a broader philosophical sense, eros applied to every form of aesthetic desire, which means all forms of attraction based on the beauty or worth of the object. We love music that sounds beautiful to our ears and therefore imparts satisfaction to our sense of sound—eros. We love a piece of art because it is beautiful to our eyes and therefore imparts visual pleasure—eros. We love a well-prepared meal because it is composed in such a manner as to delight our taste buds—eros. A man loves a woman because her form is beautiful to his eyes and holds potential to bring him physical pleasure—eros. A woman loves a man because his personality gratifies her sense of personal self-esteem—eros.

Not surprisingly, a high divorce rate and/or a high incidence of infidelity may be expected in a culture dominated by eros. It is inevitable that the aesthetic value of any given person will wane or be surpassed by a competing attraction.

And yet, it is also immediately obvious that eros isn't all bad. Or we might say, eros isn't bad in and of itself. What could possibly be wrong with discerning the beauty of an object and being attracted to that beauty? After all, God is the originator of all beauty and the architect of the human sensory system by which we are able to see, hear, smell, taste, and touch the good things He has made. The love of beauty and goodness was built into human nature by the Creator Himself. We will explore the legitimate pleasure dimension of God's love in the next two chapters. For now we need to wrap our minds around the theological implications of eros in its fallen form as a self-focused kind of love.

God Through Eros Eyes
Love that is outwardly focused with an inward motive—desire for you with primary reference to me—isn't just the benign topic of countless song lyrics. It is, in fact, a fundamental belief system, a paradigm of reality that drives what we assume to be true of God. The question becomes, what form does religion take in an eros paradigm? What does God look like through eros eyes?

Eros as we have just described it was seen by the Greeks as the exercise of "vulgar" or "earthly" eros, because they believed that there is a more elevated form of eros in man, a "spiritual" or "heavenly" eros. And that spiritual eros may be disciplined to channel human desire toward the heavenly idea of ultimate beauty rather than toward lower, sensual objects of attraction.

As a most basic definition, eros is love for the beautiful and the good. In its low, vulgar form, eros pursues whatever gratifies the senses: food, art, music, cinema, youthfulness, sex, adventure, sport, fitness, poetry, and the like—anything to stimulate and satisfy the body, the mind and the emotions.

But all of this earthly beauty and goodness, says Plato, is merely evidence of an absolute beauty and goodness to which we may ascend if we will channel our desires away from the earthly toward the heavenly. Sounds kind of okay so far, doesn't it? But here is where the eros conception of love moves from the secular form to take on a spiritual form that is utterly foreign to the revelation of God's character in Christ. In both applications the focus remains inward. Secular self-love merely gives way to a spiritual self-love with higher aspirations.

For Plato, and for major segments of "Christianity" that follow his lead, God exists in an impassible state (without passion). God knows nothing like desire, and most certainly He has no regard for mankind, because God completely transcends all outward focus. God desires nothing because God has all He desires. In God there is no want, no longing, no hope, no yearning, no love for anything or anyone outside of Himself. God is Pure Self and therefore exists in a state of pure self-gratification. This is why Plato could say, "A god holds no intercourse with a man, but by means of this intermediary [by which he means eros] all intercourse and discourse between gods and men is carried on" (Plato, *Symposium*, p. 203). By this, Plato means that God does not reach with desire down to man. If contact is to be had, it must occur from the human side, and eros is the bridge or ladder by which man may ascend to God. In Plato's view, God is utterly egocentric, totally absorbed in Himself, and void of anything like other-centeredness. All desire lies on the human side and therefore all the movement in the venture of elevation (or "salvation" in the Christianized sense of Plato's philosophy) must logically lie with the human. So not only is God viewed as egocentric, but man must also assume an egocentric position in his spiritual quest. God is self-love and man's only hope of salvation lies in self-love, as well.

By taking Plato's eros philosophy into its theology, various human-centered doctrines and practices have been incorporated into Christianity. The amalgamation began in earnest from about the 5th century onward. A large branch of "Christendom" immersed itself in what came to be known as "asceticism," which involves renouncing material comforts for habits of austere self-discipline in order to attain higher and higher levels of spiritual improvement. Monasteries, convents and cloisters multiplied. Various orders of ascetics (monks and nuns) were established. Doctrines and practices were developed to accommodate and mirror the eros brand of spirituality:

• Penance—acts of self-mortification or punishments that are imposed on one's self or prescribed by the priest in order to prove repentance genuine or in exchange for absolution.

• Indulgences—to receive remission of a temporal punishment that is still due for sin in exchange for money or a prescribed act of self-denial.

• Flagellation—to whip one's self, or to voluntarily receive such from another person, as punishment for sin or to impel one's self toward good works.

• Celibacy—to remain unmarried and, therefore, sexually abstinent in order to suppress earthly desires for the purpose of attaining a higher spiritual state and for securing merit.

• Purgatory—a place or state in which the souls of those not condemned to external torment, but not fit for heaven, undergo suffering for the purpose of purging and expiating sin.

All of these teachings and practices, as well as a number of others, were simply the logical outworking of the eros picture of God adopted from Greek philosophy. The bottom line of eros theology is that God does not move toward man, because God cannot love anything beneath Himself. If eros is the love of beauty and goodness, and if God is sheer eros in its most elevated form, then God can only love those who are beautiful and good. Since we are below God in beauty and goodness, it follows that an elevation to beauty and goodness must occur in man as the pre-condition to union with God. Man must go up to the plane where God is, with no help or even interest from God. And so it becomes clear that an eros-based spirituality is a man-centered orientation, or what is called "salvation by works."

This view of God and of salvation was not invented by the Greeks. It simply reached an intellectually developed plateau with their philosophers. It is the view common to all religions and cultures down through history (with only one exception, to which we are about to give our attention). The basic idea that God must be reached by man, that God must be appeased by man, that God's favor must be merited by goodness attained by man, in whatever language or configuration it may take, is the only way man is capable of viewing his relation to God while under the spell of self-centeredness. Our only conceivable hope for deliverance would be for God Himself to break the power of the lie by actually doing what our carnal logic tells us He would never do: condescend to us, desire us, reach out and down to us in a radical, paradigm-shifting demonstration of self-sacrificing love.

And this is precisely what God has done in Christ.

Paradigm Shift

God's love, as vowed by covenant to Abraham and then personified in Christ, is of an entirely different character than the eros love of the Greeks and of all the man-centered religions of antiquity. It is so utterly different, in fact, that Paul, discerning the contrast, specifically called attention to the problem the Christ-revelation of God would pose for the Greek mind:

"The message of the cross is foolishness to those who are perishing, but to us who are being saved it is the power of God. For it is written: 'I will destroy the wisdom of the wise, and bring to nothing the understanding of the prudent.' Where is the wise? Where is the scribe? Where is the disputer of this age? Has not God made foolish the wisdom of this world? For since, in the wisdom of God, the world through wisdom did not know God, it pleased God through the foolishness of the message preached to save those who believe. For Jews request a sign, and Greeks seek after wisdom; but we preach Christ crucified, to the Jews a stumbling block and to the Greeks foolishness, but to those who are called, both Jews and Greeks, Christ the power of God and the wisdom of God. Because the foolishness of God is wiser than men, and the weakness of God is stronger than men" (1 Corinthians 1:18-25).

Something was manifested in Christ that was scandalous to the Hellenized Jews of Paul's day and absolute foolishness to the Greek way of thinking. That something was a categorically different kind of love. It was the idea that God is composed of a quality of love that would put Him voluntarily on a cross. The concept was so distinct from eros that only a complete paradigm shift would be sufficient to accommodate its acceptance. And according to Paul, the cross intends to escort the human mind into just such a paradigm shift. We are asked to believe that there on the cross, bleeding and dying, is the most powerful and exalted being in the universe—none other than almighty God.

Here is God displayed in outreaching passion,

God in the throes of intense desire for man,

God condescending to the lowest place imaginable for sheer love of others above Himself.

No more radical inversion of reality could be conceivable for the Greek mind, or for any human mind for that matter.

Of all people, Friedrich Nietzsche, the famous (or infamous) atheist who declared, "God is dead," understood, at least momentarily, the scandalous glory of the apostle's view of God:

"Modern men, hardened as they are to all Christian terminology, no longer appreciate the horrible extravagance which, for all ancient taste, lay in the paradox of the formula, 'God on the cross.' Never before had there been anywhere such an audacious inversion, never anything so terrifying, so challenging and challengeable, as this formula; it promised a transvaluation of all ancient values" (Friedrich Nietzsche, *Beyond Good and Evil*, p. 46; translated into English and quoted in Anders Nygren, *Agape and Eros*, p. 202).

In other words, the idea that God is of such a character that He would die on a cross totally contradicts every human value system ever conceived. So absolutely contrary is the cross to all human notions of what God ought to be like, that the cross constitutes a total inversion of the human conception of reality. The idea that God would actually love those beneath Him more than His own life is simply a horrible extravagance beyond comprehension.

If I could, I would remind Nietzsche that Paul, while preaching "God on a cross," did not hesitate to confess that the idea, indeed, "surpasses knowledge" (Ephesians 3:19, NIV).

In fact, the love of God revealed in Christ is so completely opposite to the broken eros love that devalues the human heart's natural picture of God, that the apostles found it necessary to employ an entirely different word than eros in order to preach Christ.

A Vocabulary Revolution
Eros was the Greek word for love in common usage at the time of Christ and the apostles. And yet, amazingly, eros is not used one time in the New Testament. Instead, the apostles adopted a rare word almost never employed. The word they chose was agape.

Agape could not be called a linguistic invention of the apostles, but it was definitely a deliberate vocabulary revolution on their part. The apostles were Hebrews. They were well acquainted with hesed as the key Hebrew word for God's covenantal love. They were also very familiar with the Greco-Roman culture that surrounded them and its obsession with eros or self-gratifying love. The clash between the two concepts was obvious. So these first followers of Jesus deliberately kept eros out of the vocabulary of the gospel. But they needed a word to effectively communicate the covenant-keeping character of God, a word that would serve as a Greek equivalent of hesed. Agape was chosen because, while obscure to popular culture, it carried the idea of altruism, benevolence, or unconditional goodwill. Because agape was not favored by the mainstream culture, it could be co-opted and owned by the gospel of Christ.

If hesed is the Old Testament word [idea] used to tell us that God is totally actuated by faithful love, then agape is the New Testament word chosen by the apostles to describe the same truth as it came to full expression in the person of Jesus Christ. *Hesed* informs us that the God encountered by the prophets is of such a good character that He will keep His covenant of love at any and all cost to Himself. *Agape* informs us that this surprisingly beautiful God followed through on His word all the way to the point of complete self-sacrifice.

Agape is categorically different than eros.

The declaration, God is agape (1 John 4:8), is the only total identity statement made about God in the whole Bible. It is, in fact, the only comprehensive, all-encompassing declaration regarding the divine character that may be made with a single word in the form of a noun. The declaration is not "God is *loving*," but rather, "God is *love*."

While the Bible tells us that God is *just*, it never says God is *justice*. God is said to be *merciful*, but never *mercy*. God is *kind*, but not *kindness*. *Gentle*, but not *gentleness*. *Patient*, but not *patience*. *Holy*, but not *holiness*. Love, in the unilateral and passionate agape sense, stands alone as the only word that encompasses the totality of God's being. Everything that is true of God is true of God because God is love. God is *just* in all His ways due to the fact that God is love, because *justice* is an attribute of love. God is *merciful* due to the fact that God is love, because *mercy* is an attribute of love. And the same is true of every other divine character trait. Agape is not one trait in a list of others. Rather, it is the complete whole of who and what manner of person God is.

Paul paints for us a full-featured picture of agape. Because God is love, each time the apostle uses the word love we may just as easily insert the word God:

"God is patient, God is kind. God does not envy, He does not boast, He is not proud. God is not rude, He is not self-seeking, He is not easily angered, He keeps no record of wrongs. God does not delight in evil but rejoices with the truth. God always protects, always trusts, always hopes, always perseveres" (1 Corinthians 13:4-7, PT).

All of this beautifully descriptive expounding on the character of agape, which is the character of God, leads up to one superb declaration Paul has saved for the climax of His song: "Love never fails" (verse 8).

In those three simple but powerful words, the meaning of agape is distilled to its essence. Whatever the circumstances may be, God just keeps on being what and who He is—changelessly faithful.

Agape Moves
But God's agape is more than a word to be defined with more words. It is the radically aggressive action of God's self-sacrifice demonstrated in the incarnation, life, death, and resurrection of Christ. John declares, "by this we know love [agape], because He laid down His life for us" (1 John 3:16). It is the downward-going, self-giving action of God's heart that most perfectly defines His love. When the Bible says "God is love" (1 John 4:8), it most emphatically does not mean that God is attracted to any aesthetic beauty or moral goodness in us from which He seeks to gain personal gratification. The truth is much more humbling and powerful than that.

First, and foremost, "God is love" in a perfectly unilateral (one-way) sense. He doesn't love us because of us, but rather because of Him. Not because we offer Him the prospect of pleasure or satisfaction, but in spite of the fact that we have brought Him tremendous heartache and pain. Not because we're good, but because He's good.

Secondly, "God is love" in a perfectly sensitive or passionate sense as well. He does not exist without desire for those outside of Himself, but rather full of desire for all who are the objects of His unilateral love. Within God's nature there is a concrete reality of other-centeredness.

God's unilateral love does most certainly generate a bilateral relationship between the human recipient and Himself. This is due entirely to the powerful effect His love exerts on our hearts. But the relationship does not begin on a mutual premise. We do not first act toward God in a positive manner that elicits a positive response from Him. He is already positive toward us simply because that's the kind of person He is. His love works in the opposite direction to eros. It moves in reverse of fallen human love. Nietzsche called it an "inversion" and a "transvaluation" of all human value systems. The concept feels backwards to us, upside down, inside out. The natural egocentric consciousness of the human mind automatically assumes that self must figure large into the salvation equation. The idea that God's love must be merited is satisfying to our sense of self-worth. But agape informs us that God's love is self-contained and not in any sense aroused or generated by anything we may do to earn it. His love is not dependent upon what we have to offer Him. God loves us because God is love, and there's a big period there.

This is both greatly to our benefit and very humbling. In our fallen condition we want to be loved based on our attractiveness and virtues, on the premise of what we have to offer. Nobody is inclined to enter a relationship in which someone might say, in so many words, "You're ugly, stupid, and annoying, but I love you anyway. Will you marry me?" Of course the answer is, *No!* Within the realm of human relationships, encumbered as we are with the self-centered dysfunctions of the Fall, we love with reference to ourselves and we want to be loved with reference to ourselves. But within the realm of the human relationship to God, the fact is that we are ugly, stupid, and annoying, and that's an understatement. We are fallen, rebellious, defiant, selfish individuals who have imposed immeasurable pain upon the heart of God. If God's love were dependant on attractiveness in us for its engagement, we would all be hopelessly lost. Yes, it is humbling to realize that God loves us in spite of the fact that we are so manifestly unlovable and undeserving, but we are very fortunate that this is the case.

So then, God is love with finality. There is no sense in which the sentence may be completed, "God is love if . . . ," or, "God is love when . . . " No. God is love, *period*, without condition or alteration. Nothing external to God motivates, generates, or actualizes His love. Whatever you may do by way of bad deeds, God will not cease loving you or love you less, even to the point of following you to your eternal destruction. Whatever you may do by way of good deeds, God will not love you more. The moment we view God's love as in any sense being conditioned, elicited, won, merited, altered, earned, or aroused by anything outside of Himself, we have departed from agape and have now conceived of God as eros, which is to conceive of God as egocentric. God is now dependent on us rather than independent in Himself for the state of His being.

God is the desire of my heart for only one reason, and that is because I am the desire of His heart. I desire Him because He desires me. If He did not want me, there is nothing in me that would want Him or that would be capable of ascending to Him. My desire for God is an echo of His for me. He is in the position of initiator, pursuer, and aggressor.

The flower looks like it opens up and reaches out to the sun, but in fact the sun is first shining its energy-giving light upon the flower so that it is merely responsive to the sun. Likewise, the human heart does not naturally seek God. It is not innately good in its desires. We seek God because His unilateral love is exerting a drawing influence on our souls.

Draw the contrast:

Eros love is desire that begins from a position of emptiness. Agape love is desire that begins from a position of fullness.

Eros is inwardly focused desire—self-centered. Agape is outwardly focused desire—other-centered.

Eros seeks to acquire. Agape gives.

Eros loves the beautiful and the good. Agape loves in spite of ugliness and badness.

Eros is an ascending motion. Agape is a descending motion.

Eros is (imagines itself to be) unilateral from the human side in order to arouse response from God. Agape is unilateral from God's side in order to arouse response in man.

Eros seeks beauty and pleasure in its object. Agape generates beauty and pleasure in its object.

Eros envisions a merit-based salvation. Agape is a grace-based salvation.

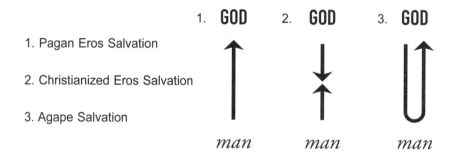

1. Pagan Eros Salvation

2. Christianized Eros Salvation

3. Agape Salvation

Jesus has come all the way down to where we are, taken us into Himself, and then lifted us up to the very pinnacle of reality at the right hand of the Father.

In Ephesians 2, Paul explains the marvelous truth of the matter. He first states our position in the situation. We were "dead in trespasses and sins" (verse 1). By "dead" he means completely bankrupt of moral goodness and absolutely inactive in relation to God. Our lives have consisted of "fulfilling the desires of the flesh and of the mind" (verse 3). There is no sense of innate human desire for God here, no spiritual eros in us moving us toward God. In our natural state we are dead to God and aggressive in selfishness. Then Paul gives the good news:

"But because of His great love [agape] for us, God, who is rich in mercy, made us alive with Christ even when we were dead in transgressions—it is by grace you have been saved. And God raised us up with Christ and seated us with Him in the heavenly realms in Christ Jesus, in order that in the coming ages He might show the incomparable riches of His grace, expressed in His kindness to us in Christ Jesus" (verses 4-7, NIV).

Agape moved God toward us when we had no inclination to move toward Him. And the movement He made was of a monumental distance. When Paul says "God raised us up with Christ and seated us with Him in the heavenly realms in Christ Jesus," he has the incarnation, death, resurrection, and ascension of Christ in mind. Astoundingly, according to Paul, fallen humanity was somehow included in that entire circuit. Jesus became human. He died on the cross bearing our human nature. He came forth from the grave as much a human being as He was when He went into the grave. Then He ascended to the heavenly realm as a human being. Quite literally, a human being now occupies the throne of the universe at the right hand of the Father. The fact that He is also fully divine does not negate the fact that He is also fully human. This means that the entire salvation project was accomplished by God in Christ one hundred percent by virtue of His agape love. While we were dead in sin, He achieved the salvation of the human race.

Because of the unilateral nature of God's love, Paul informs us that there is only one appropriate and effectual response. Salvation by works is strictly ruled out by the logic of agape. Since God came down, there is no point in striving to ascend to Him. Since God already loves us, there is no reason to try to earn His love. Since salvation is accomplished in Christ, there is no logic in trying to merit salvation. The only response that makes any sense at all in the agape paradigm is faith. Paul explains:

"For it is by grace you have been saved, through faith—and this not from yourselves, it is the gift of God—not by works, so that no one can boast. For we are God's workmanship, created in Christ Jesus to do good works, which God prepared in advance for us to do" (verses 8-10, NIV).

Astounding, huh!

Reality is something you *believe*, not something you *manufacture*. Because human salvation is a historical fact in Christ—a concrete reality—the gospel calls upon us to believe it. By definition, faith is a *responsive* action of the mind, not an *actualizing* action. Faith *believes* facts; it doesn't *make* facts. That is why faith is the only appropriate way to enter into the salvation of Christ. Our part is to allow the power of God's agape to transform us. Even our response is His work in us.

Once we enter by faith, we realize we are "God's workmanship, created in Christ Jesus to do good works, which God prepared in advance for us to do." Agape inevitably activates moral movement in those who believe it. Within the experiential parameters of the faith response to God's agape, as opposed to the works spirituality of eros, we become a new creation of God's making. God's love authors a new life of good works in us, a life free from the pagan anxiety of trying to earn God's favor, and empowered by the fact that we already have it. By virtue of its unconditional nature, God's love generates response in the form of gratitude, awe, appreciation, motivation, and a general sense of blown-away adoration. Agape is a creative force—a restorative, healing, life-giving power.

Which leads us right into the incredible realization that God's unilateral love invariably generates a returning current of desire and love from our hearts to His. In other words, it's so fast and powerful and alive that it's reciprocal.

Quick, next chapter!

fourteen

R E C I P R O C A L

*I*llustrating the fact that space is curved Albert Einstein is reported to have said, "If you had a telescope powerful enough, you could see the back of your head."

It is a curious observation that pretty much everything in the universe, as well as the universe as a whole, is round and rotational. Every functional system is composed of interacting parts that move in and out of one another in circular motion, and every individual system then relates interactively to other systems to form larger systems, wheel within wheel within wheel of giving and receiving action. As the frontiers of science expand, this one shape and this one pattern of movement shows up everywhere we look on every level.

In his brilliant book, *Linked*, University of Notre Dame professor of physics, Albert-László Barabási persuades us that "Everything is connected to everything else." He demonstrates chapter by chapter that "our biological existence, social world, economy, and religious traditions tell a compelling story of interrelatedness. . . . Today we increasingly recognize that nothing happens in isolation. Most events and phenomena are connected, caused by, and interacting with a huge number of other pieces of a complex universal puzzle. We have come to see that we live in a small world, where everything is linked to everything else. We are witnessing a revolution in the making as scientists from all different disciplines discover that complexity has a strict architecture" (pp. 5, 7).

The "strict architecture" that Barabási and "scientists from all different disciplines" are discovering just happens to be the strict architectural plan we find explained throughout the Bible. The whole universe at all levels is structured after the pattern of the heart of the communitarian God of love who designed it all. "For since the creation of the world," Paul says, "His invisible attributes are clearly seen, being understood by the things that are made, even His eternal power and Godhead" (Romans 1:20). According to the apostle, the relational nature of God—God as a triune fellowship of other-centeredness—is evident in nature itself as a reflective medium.

New Movements In The Soul

This chapter is a graduated return to the theme of roundness and rotation we began to explore in our chapter regarding the governmental structure of God's Kingdom. Only now we will give our attention to the circle-pattern as it occurs at the most intimate level of reality.

Between hearts.

Between the human heart and the divine heart, more specifically.

As we have already discovered, God is the epicenter of all things good and beautiful (James 1:17). "God is love" in the most primary, original, and eternally alive sense. He was never without love, never acquired it from any more fundamental source, nor did He ever generate it from some lower form to a higher. God is love in the *noun* sense. Love composes the pervasive essence of the total divine identity. Everything else that's true of God—all the *adjectives* and *verbs*—is true of God because God is love. And so the circle of life and love begins with God. Love pours from God like a massive, mighty river of fire.

As God's love flows out of Himself in the tangible form of self-giving deeds, it seeks access to human hearts. It pursues living beings that have the capacity to discern it, to feel it, and to volitionally respond to it.

Like you, for example.

Once access is granted (recall that He "knocks"), the effect of God's love is to create a whole new set of perceptions and emotions. The individual begins to understand that he is the object of a perfectly selfless love. It starts to dawn on his mind that he was made for higher and better things. The realization that God is full of mercy and forgiveness sinks into his heart. He begins to feel gratitude and adoration for such a God as this. A deep sense of "godly fear," holy awe, and sober reverence takes hold of him. And then—not really in succession *after* the new perceptions and emotions are formed, but more in tandem *with* them—the will begins to move in a new direction.

Away from sin toward obedience.

Away from selfishness toward love.

Away from hostility, resentment, manipulation, violation, and all forms of anti-love behavior toward "love, joy, peace, longsuffering, kindness, goodness, faithfulness, gentleness, self-control" (Galatians 5:22-23).

Relational integrity becomes the grand passion of the soul:

to love like God loves,

to be faithful like God is faithful,

to genuinely care for God and all others like God cares.

When divine desire meets human desire, a massive release of moral energy occurs.

All this new movement of the thoughts, the feelings, and the will flows in a fundamentally different direction than we've ever experienced before. The new movement is outward, whereas what we have previously known was primarily an inward orientation. The power of self-centeredness begins to be broken in our lives. We start to see God and others as of primary importance. A journey has begun in which we become less and less focused on and anxious about ourselves.

In other words, the heart returns to God. The love that flows forth from Him has now awakened the powers of the soul and generated a returning current of active love.

The Circle Made Complete In Christ

The Ten Commandments describe what the round and rotational pattern of God's love looks like in practical, relational application. The first four commandments tell us what love to God looks like in action. The remaining six commandments tell us what love to our fellow human beings looks like in action. One cannot imagine a more blissful world than one in which every member of society has a great relationship with their parents by faithfully valuing them with attitudes and actions of honor; a world in which nobody ever injures anyone else, never takes life, and never even feels hatred for anyone; a world in which every married couple is totally devoted to one another with unfailing fidelity; a world in which nobody ever takes what belongs to another; a world in which every person is completely honest and trustworthy; a world in which all are content with what they have, and feel no desire for what belongs to anyone else; and a world in which every person knows and loves and worships God with adoring devotion.

That's the kind of world the Ten Commandments envision.

In other words, the Ten Commandments are a law of relational faithfulness. That's why the Bible repeatedly refers to them with the word "covenant" (Exodus 34:28; Deuteronomy 4:13; 9:10-11). "Covenant" means relational faithfulness, and the Ten Commandments are a concise and yet comprehensive explanation of the things relationally faithful people do and don't do.

There is a huge problem, however.

The covenant has been broken by humanity. "All have sinned and fall short of the glory of God" (Romans 3:23). According to the Bible, "sin is transgression of the law" (1 John 3:4, KJV) and "love is the fulfillment of the law" (Romans 13:10). If God's law is the covenant, and if sin is transgression of the law, then sin is the breaking of the covenant of love in our relationships with God and one another. Sin is therefore the failure to love, meaning the failure to live for God and all others above and before self. But rather than abandon us to our unfaithfulness, God has chosen to remain faithful to us, and thereby restore us to lives of relational faithfulness. The word "covenant" describes the course of action God has taken to achieve this plan.

Sometimes the Bible draws a contrast between an old covenant and a new covenant. From God's side of the relationship there is only one covenant. Scripture often speaks in a singular grammar of the "everlasting covenant" (Hebrews 13:20; Genesis 9:16; 17:17; Isaiah 55:3; Ezekiel 16:60-63; Revelation 14:6). There is a sense in which there is really only one eternal reality of covenant, which is manifested in seven historic phases:

First, there is the covenant of faithful love that existed for all eternity past between the Father, Son, and Holy Spirit (Genesis 1:1; Deuteronomy 6:4; John 17:24; 1 John 5:7).

Second, the covenant of divine love was externalized in creation. God made other beings to share in the glorious joy of His love (Genesis 1:26).

Third, the Father, Son, and Holy Spirit engaged in the covenant of peace among themselves—to save fallen humanity at any cost (Isaiah 54:10).

Fourth, God promised Adam and Eve that a warrior would be sent to crush the kingdom of evil and win salvation for mankind (Genesis 3:15).

Fifth, in the face of a nearly universal violence that threatened the extinction of the human race, God faithfully intervened with the

Flood and entered into covenant with Noah (Genesis 6).

Sixth, God entered into covenant with Abraham, Isaac, and Jacob, and thus with the nation of Israel (Genesis 12-22).

Seventh, through Israel, the covenant people, God finally entered human history in the flesh to fulfill all the promises made at every stage of the everlasting covenant. In the divine human person of Jesus Christ total covenantal faithfulness was achieved (Isaiah 42:6; Luke 1:72-73, 77-79). "For all the promises of God in Him are Yes, and in Him Amen" (2 Corinthians 1:20).

The Son of God was given to the human race as the pledge of covenantal faithfulness (Isaiah 42:6; Daniel 9:24-27; 11:22). Jesus fulfilled every feature of the covenant in that He proved faithful to *God as man*, and faithful to *man as God*. He is the grand identity bridge between God and humanity. He was in actuality fully God and fully human.

As God, He loved us without retaliation to the point of death (Romans 5:8; Philippians 2:5-8; 1 Peter 2:21-24).

As man, He lived in perfect obedience to God's law of love to the point of death (Romans 8:2-4; Philippians 2:5-8).

When He died, having maintained this bilateral faithfulness, the covenant was sealed, confirmed and ratified in blood (Hebrews 9:12-18; 10:14; 12:14).

The *hesed* love of the covenant promise, and the *agape* love of the covenant promise fulfilled in Christ, are distilled to their essence in Paul's one line declaration, "Love never fails" (1 Corinthians 13:8). That's the whole point. God's love is constant, changeless, unstoppable. Whatever the external circumstances are, divine love keeps right on being what it is—faithful, devoted, committed.

In fulfillment of all that the prophets had written, God the Son entered our world incarnate, revealed the truth about God, suffered and died as the consummate act of God's self-giving love and rose from the dead on the third day victorious over all sin, guilt, and unfaithfulness.

God did all of this in order "to perform the mercy promised to our fathers and to remember His holy covenant, the oath which He swore to our father Abraham. . . . To give knowledge of salvation to His people by the remission of their sins, through the tender mercy of our God, with which the Dayspring from on high has visited us; to give light to those who sit in darkness and the shadow of death, to guide our feet in the way of peace" (Luke 1:72-73, 77-79).

The way God's covenantal love operates is to first act toward us, for us, on our behalf, in absolute self-giving devotion. This was totally achieved in Christ as an historical event. Secondly, God's covenantal love intends to capture our attention and draw us into covenant response. It is a proposal looking for a "Yes!"

The overall goal of the covenant is to reestablish relational faithfulness as the only mode of interaction throughout all of creation. To achieve this, the self-centered motive of the human heart must somehow be eradicated and replaced with an other-centered motive.

Jesus articulated this goal beautifully as He prayed for His followers, "that they all may be one [relationally faithful in love], as You, Father, are in Me, and I in You; that they also may be one in Us. . . . O Righteous Father! The world has not known You, but I have known You; and these have known that You sent Me. And I have declared to them Your name, and will declare it, that the love [agape] with which You have loved Me may be in them, and I in them" (John 17:21, 25-26).

Can you imagine!

All God wants is to reincorporate you and me into the beautiful love relationship that the Father, Son and Holy Spirit enjoy.

Externally Imposed Or Internally Formed
Okay, so we see that there is a sense in which the covenant is a

singular, "everlasting" reality. It is simply the truth of God's faithful character unfolding in a continuum of stages. But from another angle the Bible speaks of two covenants—the old and the new.

Paul explains the old covenant versus the new covenant in terms of an externally imposed law of "letter" versus an internally integrated law of "spirit." He says that those who make the transition from the one to the other "are delivered from the law" so that they "serve in newness of spirit, and not in oldness of the letter" (Romans 7:6, KJV). Another translation says, "And now you can really serve God; not in the old way, mechanically obeying a set of rules, but in the new way, with all your hearts and minds" (Tay).

What Paul is describing here is two totally different ways of perceiving and relating to God and His law. The old covenant way is to see God as imposing a merely behavior-regulating law. We obey the law outwardly from a sense of obligation in order to escape punishment and gain salvation. Therefore, the underlying motive is a self-serving fear, because God is viewed as an arbitrary slave master demanding behavioral conformity in exchange for His favor. The heart remains unchanged.

By contrast, the new covenant way is to understand that God is seeking access to the heart in order to affect a total transformation of motive and character. The law is written on our hearts and minds as an internal law of self-giving love. There is no sense of merit or exchange. We don't obey the law in order to escape punishment and secure salvation, but rather because we have been radically changed by the love of God manifested for us in Christ.

Earlier in Romans, Paul explains the premise of the new covenant and how it becomes activated in our lives. That premise is the self-sacrificing love of God demonstrated by the death of Jesus on our behalf, not because we earned or deserved such love, but rather "while we were still sinners" (Romans 5:6-8). The new covenant is grounded in the cross as the historical event by which God proved the unconditional, unilateral nature of His love. Arising from that premise, the new covenant becomes experientially activated in our lives by means of faith. Faith alone can avail to establish the new covenant in our hearts, because in order for God's love to gain access to our hearts, it must be intelligently understood, believed, and acted upon. And that's what faith does. Faith is not a blind leap in the dark possessing no evidence. Rather, faith is founded upon the historic revelation of God's love in Christ.

Faith first involves receiving new information that constructs in the mind a new and true picture of God's character. This is why Paul portrays the cross of Christ as a *demonstration* (Romans 5:8). It puts on display the specific quality of God's love as a love that precedes any good works we might do to earn it. Once we assess God's love, faith involves believing the new revelation to be true. Therefore, faith is a rational, intelligent action of the mind, not an irrational leap in the dark. Once the truth of God's love is believed, faith then acts in glad response to the truth. Therefore, Paul speaks of "the obedience *of* faith" (Romans 16:26, KJV) and "obedience *to* the faith" (Romans 1:5). Obedience to God's law of love is the practical manifestation of new covenant faith. But it is not a mechanical, salvation-centered obedience. Faith-generated obedience has a specific quality to it. First, it is not merely externally rendered, but arises from within. Paul says of the new covenant Christian, "You obeyed from the heart" (Romans 6:17). Secondly, faith-generated obedience is not motivated by fear of punishment and hope of reward, but rather by the love of Christ (Romans 5:1-5; 13:10; Galatians 2:20; 5:5-6; 2 Corinthians 3:14-21).

In other words, as God's covenantal love flows from Him into us, it becomes reciprocal.

Love begets love.

That's just what it does.

"We love Him because He first loved us" (1 John 4:19).

fifteen

R I V E R

According to King David, a "river" of "pleasures" flows from God. The poet king says that those who "drink" from this river will be "abundantly satisfied" (Psalm 36:8).

We might say, fulfilled to the maximum level.

There is some sense in which God is the source of an eternally cascading flood of delights. Whatever this river is, its properties are so powerful and refreshing that David declares it to be "the fountain of life" (verse 9). But we don't need to wonder or guess what the river is made of. David tells us twice in his song:

"How precious is Your lovingkindness [hesed], O God!" (verse 7).

And again:

"Oh, continue Your lovingkindness [hesed] to those who know You" (verse 10).

The river of pleasure that surges forth non-stop from God is none other than His faithful, self-giving love.

This is where agape stands apart from eros in its broken form, and yet includes what may be regarded as an eros that is whole and pure as a legitimate dimension of agape.

Aesthetic love, or the capacity to take pleasure in the beauties of others, is a righteous and healthy dimension of a full-orbed agape love. While agape is not deterred by the ugliness of sin, it is certainly not gratified or fulfilled by sin either. Agape is not actualized in God by the worth of its object, but it does create worth in its object. God's love has beauty in mind as an objective, but not as a motive. Agape includes an immutable aspect and an emotive aspect. It is decidedly proactive, aggressively pursuant, fervently desirous, and all the while utterly unconditional. We most certainly are not beautiful of heart when God first loves us, which is a polite way of saying we are, in fact, very ugly of heart when He first loves us. But it is also true that God loves to an end, and it is a wonderful and exalted end. God loves us to the beautifying of our hearts and lives (Ephesians 5:25-27; Isaiah 61:3).

Broken Eros
Of itself, by itself, as a lone impulse, eros takes on the hideous form of pure selfishness. And this is precisely the form it has taken in the Fall of mankind. All self-obsessed pleasures are inverted perversions of good pleasures designed by God for our elevation and enjoyment. Eros must be subsumed within agape to have a valid form of existence and expression.

The problem eros poses in its fallen form is deeper than merely its appetite for pleasure.

Pleasure *of* itself is not wrong, but pleasure *for* itself is.

Eros belongs to God in its original form as one dimension of His full-orbed love. It is rooted in the divine character and was built into human nature as part of God's plan. God is the author of all true beauties, and God is the one who encoded into the human system the capacity to enjoy them. But in the divine order of values, eros is only a valid aspect of His full-spectrum love when it occurs as the natural by-product of other-centeredness. Pleasure is only legitimate as the residual effect of self-giving relationship, but not as a primary pursuit. Pleasure for pleasure's sake is anything but love. God is not completely antithetical to eros, but rather eros is only what God meant it to be when it takes its place of design as agape's fruit. Pleasure derives from love, but it is not love itself.

Agape says that God is a triune social unit involving both Self and Other, in which each self always moves toward the others. Each member of the divine community is self-deferring. That is the secret and source of their joy. Within the holy divine circle each one of the Eternal Three lives for the others. They please one another, delight in one another, and magnify the beauty of one another. The Bible teaches us that God is an emotive being. God does feel. Desire is experientially known to God. Pleasure does occur within the sacred precincts of the Godhead, but it is a specific quality of pleasure that derives from their self-giving love for one another. Self-concern is non-existent within God's social reality. God does not live in an austere, impassible, ridged, heavy mood of reserve, but rather in an endless ecstasy of relational glory. We can only conclude, then, that God is the epicenter of all true and selfless pleasure.

Therefore, man is invited into absolute other-centeredness as his normal mode of existence, for that is how God lives, and that is how God made man to live in the beginning.

The Bible teaches that human beings were designed by God for an Edenic existence. Eden means pleasure. Just look at the human being objectively. Our bodies and minds were obviously engineered for pleasure. Our senses are clearly meant to be pleasure receptacles. We perceive, emote, taste, touch, hear, smell, and see with enormous potential for pleasure. But there is a deep secret to the way the Designer designed us. It's not a secret because God has deliberately hidden it, but because the truth has become a strange and dark enigma to us in our fallen condition.

The secret is other-centeredness.

With pristine innocence, the glory of the unfallen Adam and Eve lay in the fact that they only saw one another, thought of one another, felt for one another, and behaved with reference to one another. Their love was free of self-interest (which is almost beyond our comprehension), and it was precisely because they were each totally oriented toward the other that their existence was so rich with pleasure. The pleasure they enjoyed possessed meaning without self as the center of reference. Each one experienced pleasure as the residual effect of being genuinely loved by the other.

That's Eden.

That's pleasure given, not gotten, and gotten in the giving.

It's so circular.

So beautifully circular.

If we believe the story told in Genesis 1 and 2, we must accept that God is the author of pleasure. Somehow that idea doesn't register naturally in our minds. We don't generally think of God as the inventor of pleasure. But He is. Sin is simply (though not simplistically) a hijack operation. It jumps onboard and drives the human body and mind into self-serving behavior patterns that give the illusion of fulfillment while destroying the fine machinery of the soul. Whereas love is a thriving, life-giving exercise of the human operating system, sin is love in reverse. Sin is pleasure sought for pleasure's sake.

In our fallen condition, we have become creatures of carnal, self-serving pleasure. As such, we scarcely can comprehend the idea of a kind of pleasure that occurs organically within the framework of serving others with no regard for self. Our fallen condition makes strange the ways of God, although they are nothing short of absolute normality for the unfallen universe beyond our crippled planet. We human beings are broken. We don't function the way we were made to. Something is deeply and horribly wrong with us. Our world is a radiant beauty caught in the throes of a heart-wrenching tragedy. An infinite sadness hangs over our world like a thick winter fog. And yet, a glorious potential is evident as we examine the shapes and patterns that underlie the pain.

Paul says our problem is that we are "carnally minded" (Romans 8:6), by which he means we are fundamentally oriented toward ourselves. Earlier in Romans he defines our fallen condition with the word "self-seeking" (Romans 2:8). That pretty much summarizes what's wrong with us. Describing the sin problem as it escalates out of control in the final segment of human history, Paul says, in "the last days . . . men will be lovers of themselves, lovers of money . . . unloving . . . lovers of pleasure rather than lovers of God" (2 Timothy 3:1-4).

But the power of our self-centeredness is broken in Christ:

"For Christ's love [agape] compels us. . . . He died for all, that those who live should no longer live for themselves but for Him who died for them and was raised again" (2 Corinthians 5:14-15, NIV).

God most certainly does love us unilaterally, but with just as definite a desire for a bilateral effect. Everything in God's creation is relationally geared by divine design.

Does God want the joyous pleasure of our love?

Absolutely!

Jesus Himself expressed to the Father His desire for our fellowship:

"Father, I desire that they also whom You gave Me may be with Me where I am" (John 17:24).

According to Paul, Christ "endured the cross, despising the shame," *yes* for our salvation, but also "for the joy that was set before Him" (Hebrews 12:2). While God's love is completely self-giving, other-centered, and unilateral in motive, He also anticipates the "joy" of fellowship with the objects of His love. He is eager to receive a returning current of love from His redeemed ones.

Outward and downward movement is characteristic of agape:

"By this we know love [agape], because He laid down His life for us" (1 John 3:16).

At the cross of Christ we witness the most massive release of divine passion ever (that's why it is called "the passion of the Christ"). In Christ we see an infinitely strong, divine desire channeled toward each individual member of the human race. Calvary is God's unequivocal, unconditional, full throttle,

"I love you!"

But He hangs there with outturned eyes, with searching gaze, and He sees you.

His love is a question that selflessly begs an answer. He longs for a returning current of desire. The divine question hangs before you aching for response:

Will you love Me back?

He would like that very much, indeed!

And yet, He'll love you still, even if you go down in flames of self-serving passion saying no to His love.

But why say no?

sixteen

C E N T E R

*O*ne time I encountered some really big love in a really small package.

She was just four years old. Each night I had noticed her sitting with her mom during a two-week seminar I was conducting. It was evident in her eyes that she actually understood some of what I was teaching. Her mom told me she tried to get little Megan to go to the children's meetings, but she insisted on attending the adult meetings, "Because I like that man," she said.

Having just finished the last lecture in the series, here she came toward me, her mother a couple steps behind to offer support for her mission. Megan came close, a piece of paper dangling in one hand by her side, the other lifted wide in a gesture of emphasis.

"Mr. Ty," she exclaimed with an intensely serious tone, "I love you with all my . . ."

She paused with a look of perplexity as if the next word was gone from her.

". . .with all my tummy," she continued with tentative confidence, pulling her hand in to rub her stomach.

"Your *heart*, sweetie," her mom coached with a whisper from behind.

"Mr. Ty, that would be all my *heart* I love you with," she recovered.

Then Megan presented her piece of art to me.

"It's a picture of you and me holding hands," she explained. "We like each other."

Did little Megan love me with *all* her heart? And if she did, was there any love left for her mom, or for anyone else in her world? This is a seriously practical question that offers a theologically rich answer. Is it possible to give all your love to more than one person?

Of course it is!

All of Megan's love, in fact, was still there in her heart for her various family members, even as she decided to love me with all of her heart as well.

Love is like that.

It's is not a divisible *quantity*, but an exponential *quality*. And this fact carries some extremely important and exciting implications. In this chapter, we will explore your place in God's infinite, intimate heart and mine as well.

One Among Billions

It is truly marvelous to understand the enormity of God's love, to know that His love is universal in its embrace of the whole world. But it is vital that we not allow the big idea of God's love for *all* to become so generalized in our thinking that we lose awareness of the personal reality of God's love for *each*.

God's love is not, in fact, a generalized attitude about nameless masses of people. Rather, it is a concentrated focus on specific persons with names and histories and current situations. God is hyperconscious of you, and maximally sensitive regarding every minute detail of your life. Everything that touches you touches Him.

But there are billions of people in the world. How could God possibly be focused on me?

By understanding the nature of love and how it operates in our finite human realm, we can grasp, at least to some degree, how it operates on an infinite scale within the divine realm.

Reason it through with me.

Imagine that you and your spouse have been more prolific than most couples. You have ten children. Of course, the first question would be, Why did you do that to yourself? But once we get past the shock of it all, the more revealing question would be, Do you divide your love up among your children, 10% for each? Is that how love operates? Or rather do you love each of them with 100% of your love?

What we're asking is whether love is a divisible quantity or an exponential quality? We could ask the question another way, Is the nature of love such that it is possible to love more than one person simultaneously with all your love?

Of course it is!

Your love expands to include all ten children. Each one of them is the object of your total love. Not one of them could take the place of any other. If one were to die, it would not be a simple matter of having another one to replace the one you've lost. Even ten more, or a thousand more, couldn't replace the one. That one, and each one, holds an exclusive place in your heart that no other can occupy, and that exclusive place just happens to be the complete whole of all the love your heart has to give.

That's how love works.

Now then, we are finite humans, and fallen at that, so the illustration will begin to break down as the numbers increase. Once you have about twenty-five children you begin to assign numbers rather than names, and you heap spaghetti in a cattle-feeding trough in the back yard and yell, "Go for it," while you lock yourself in the bathroom.

Our emotional capacity is limited.

But no such breakdown occurs for God. By virtue of the fact that God is infinite in all His capacities, He can, and does love any given number of individuals with all His love. Because God is omnipotent, there are no barriers or restrictions in the divine emotional capacity. None of His energies ever wane with expenditure. Because God is omniscient, He knows everything going on in every life at every moment with perfect awareness. Nothing escapes His notice. Because God is omnipresent, He is literally present to every person, "standing" every moment in the immediate location of every man, woman, and child.

God's omnipotence, omniscience, and omnipresence combine within His divine nature so that He has an infinite capacity for love, making His love itself the overarching omni reality of the divine being. In other words, God is not just omnipotent, omniscient, and omnipresent, He is also omnibenevolent—full of perfect passion, sensitivity, and goodwill for every person. He is the epicenter of all true, pure, and holy love—always thinking, feeling, living, and moving outward to lavish the totality of His love upon all of us and each of us. God's love is a personalized reality for each individual.

Or we could say it like this:

Because God is love, He is acutely sensitive regarding every experience that touches every life. This very moment, and every moment, you are loved by God with all His love as if you were the only person in the universe to love.

And so am I.

When you first awake in the morning, God's eyes are upon your face as if He were alone with you in the universe. You sit up and stretch, and He is aware of the aches in your joints as if your body were His own. The first time in the day that you crack a smile or laugh, He notices and resonates with your delight. If you feel frustration or emotional hurt, be those feelings ever so slight or overwhelming, He feels them all as if they were His own, and, in fact, they are His own because you belong to Him as a child belongs to a mother.

"Not a sigh is breathed, not a pain felt, not a grief pierces the soul, but the throb vibrates to the Father's heart" (E.G. White, *The Desire of Ages*, p. 356).

God's love is like a circle, the center of which is everywhere and the circumference of which is nowhere. Place your finger anywhere on the map, on any person in any home in any city of the world, and you have placed your finger on the center of God's attention. While God's love is centered on you, it is also centered on me, and on every other person in the world. While it is infinite in its scope, taking in *all*, it is intimate in its application, wholly devoted to *each*.

Nearness Yields Sensitivity
A simple illustration will serve to open our understanding to the personal nature of God's love.

First of all, take note of the fact that each one of us has various relationships with varying degrees of nearness and, therefore, with varying levels of sensitivity. We will refer to these two experiential categories as Nearness Factor and Sensitivity Quotient, each measured in relation to the other on a scale from 1 to 10. Every relationship has a Nearness Factor that yields a Sensitivity Quotient. The relationship of the two is such that the numbers will always correspond proportionally. A Nearness Factor of 1 (a guy you've never met in Siberia named Igor) will naturally only yield a Sensitivity Quotient of no more than 1, whereas a Nearness Factor of 10 (your spouse or child) will naturally yield a Sensitivity Quotient of 10.

Every human being has an inner circle of intimate relationships. I'll use myself as an example. For me the inner circle is composed of four people: my wife Sue and our three children, Amber, Jason, and Leah. Something like this:

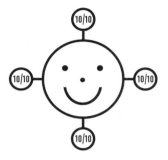
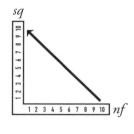

The closer I am to a person (and the same is true of you), the higher will be my sensitivity level for them. Because I have a Nearness Factor of 10 for Sue, Amber, Jason, and Leah, my Sensitivity Quotient for each one is a 10, or 100%.

If my son Jason were in a terrible accident, I would immediately change all of my plans and get to him as soon as possible. If he were suffering, I'd be deeply impacted to the point of suffering myself. That's how love operates. Conversely, if he were to experience some special blessing, like falling in love, I would be off-the-charts overjoyed.

But as a finite human being, my capacity for nearness with other human beings is limited. That is to say, my capacity for knowing individual persons is limited. I can know with intimacy only a relatively few people compared to the 6.8 billion that traverse the globe. Therefore, beyond my inner circle, all the other members of the human race take their places at various steps out from my immediate emotional vicinity. Such are the restraints of my finitude.

For example, my son Jason has a friend named Nathan. I love Nathan, but I don't know him with the level of intimacy I know

Jason. So let's say I have a Nearness Factor of 8 with Nathan, yielding a Sensitivity Quotient of 8, or 80%.

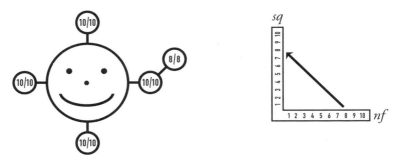

If Nathan were in a serious accident, I would be very concerned. I would pray for him. I may even call him or his family on the phone if possible. But it is not likely that I would secure a plane ticket and rush to his side. I am certain his inner circle of intimate relations would be present for him with immediacy, and I take comfort in that fact.

Now let's say Nathan has an uncle on his mother's side named Jed, and let's say I met him once at some event. With Jed I may have a Nearness Factor of 4, yielding a Sensitivity Quotient of 4. If Jed were in an accident I would not likely even call him. It's not that I don't like him, but rather that I don't know him, and sensitivity is directly linked to knowing.

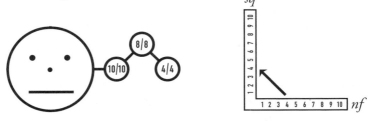

But now let's say Nathan's uncle Jed has a third cousin on his father's side named Bobby McGillicutty living in the north of Ireland. If I heard that Bobby had been in an accident, which I likely would not, I'd probably say something to my wife like, "Oh no! Poor Bobby," and a few minutes later, "Hey Sue, what's for dinner." I simply don't know the guy at all. He may as well be a polar bear at the North Pole as Bobby McGillicutty in the north of Ireland. I may have a Nearness

Factor with Bobby of no more than 2, and that's just because I know his distant nephew, and a Sensitivity Quotient of 2, and that's just because I haven't had dinner yet.

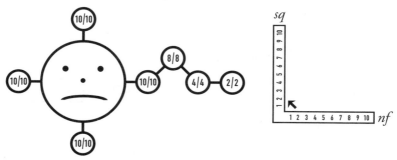

I think you see my point. The closer you are to a person, the more you'll hurt when they hurt, and the more you'll be gratified when things are going well for them. Intimacy is a factor of human social experience that calibrates our capacity for empathy. The more you love a person, the more acutely you will feel what they feel, either positive or negative.

Now think of how this works for God. Is there anyone at all that's even two steps out from God? Is there anyone God knows with less than total knowing? Absolutely not! Paul says, "He is not far from each one of us; for in Him we live and move and have our being" (Acts 17:27-28). By virtue of His omni capacities, God has a Nearness Factor of 10 with every individual on the planet, yielding a Sensitivity Quotient of 100% for each one.

This is why the Bible portrays God as a partaker in all the sufferings and joys of all human beings. Speaking of the Israelite nation during their wilderness wanderings, the prophet Isaiah declared,

"In all their affliction He was afflicted, and the Angel of His Presence saved them; in His love and in His pity He redeemed them; and He bore them and carried them all the days of old" (Isaiah 63:9).

Watching the rebellion of His people, God said through Hosea,

"How can I give you up, Ephraim? How can I hand you over, Israel . . . . My heart churns within Me; my sympathy is stirred" (Hosea 11:8).

Grasping the ultra-acute sensitivity of God's heart, King David sang,

"You keep track of all my sorrows. You have collected all my tears in Your bottle. You have recorded each one in Your book" (Psalm 56:8, NLT).

We are told in the book of Hebrews that Jesus, as our High Priest in heaven, is "touched with the feelings of our infirmities" (Hebrews 4:15, KJV), and that when human beings who once knew His love turn away from Him, "they crucify to themselves the Son of God afresh, and put Him to an open shame" (Hebrews 6:6, KJV). God knows everything. Therefore, God feels everything.

Jesus gave us an insightful look into how sensitive His love is for every human being when He said, "Inasmuch as you did it to one of the least of these My brethren, you did it to Me. . . . Inasmuch as you did not do it to one of the least of these, you did not do it to Me" (Matthew 25:40, 45).

God is so intimately connected with every person that whatever we do or don't do to anyone is done or not done to Him. He feels every mistreatment and every act of service as if done directly to Himself. The God of the Bible is the only God in all of religious thought portrayed in this way. The sensitivity of an infinite and intimate heart belongs alone to the God of the Hebrew Scriptures, to the God of *hesed* and *agape*. The Bible alone declares that "God is love" and defines that love as total other-centered goodness of character channeled with full force toward every person in the world.

Who is the person you love most in the world?

Picture their face in your mind's eye.

Think of how hurt you are when they hurt.

Think of how happy you are when they are happy.

Then build a bridge of comprehension in your mind from the way you love that person to the way God loves every person.

Ask yourself the question, Whom does God love most in this world?

Isn't the answer obvious and totally amazing?

The person God loves most is you!

And me!

And Bobby McGullicutty in the north of Ireland.

And the little boy in a small town in India whose name you'll never know.

seventeen

I N N O C E N C E

I got to thinking the other day about what I like most in this world of ours, besides Sue, that is. It didn't take me long to realize that children hold that place in my estimation. As I see it, children are the very best thing happening on planet Earth.

When Sue and I got married, we agreed to have ten or twelve kids. She wasn't totally gung-ho, but she was easily convinced. When 8lb. 10 oz. Amber came out of Sue's five-foot-three, one-hundred-and-ten pound body, she said, "How 'bout we settle for six?" The small number didn't sound good to me, but I agreed because I like her. Soon Jason came along as wide as he was tall, and Sue said, "I'd be okay with four kids." Again, I reluctantly submitted. Then Leah exited the womb in some kind of backwards or upside-down contortion with one hand tightly gripping Sue's spleen or something, and Sue said, "I'm done!" with her fingernails digging into my arm in a manner to suggest that I had better agree. "So three it is," I said with no resistance. "Now let go of my arm."

Whenever I close my eyes and think of the happiest memories tucked away in my mind, my children are always there. I see myself on a mission trip to Latvia with Amber, and she's innocent and beautiful and missing her mom. I see myself with Jason on a mountain-bike ride lost in the woods in a rainstorm, and we're laughing and dripping as we take shelter under a tree. I see myself carrying Leah on my shoulders as we hike to a waterfall, and she's giggling and banging my head saying, "Giddy up Daddy."

A Picture Of Innocence

Recently, a couple friends of mine and I were passing through a small village in Zambia where I found myself in the presence of a beautiful innocence.

Taking a rest, I was standing in the shade near a one-room mud house while my friends were inside doing some video work. About ten feet in front of me was a single strand of fence wire stretched between posts. Beyond the wire another twenty feet or so was another mud house. In front of the building there were two women washing clothing in a cauldron of water being heated on an open fire.

As I watched the execution of the mundane chore, a little girl, about five years old, came bouncing with energy out of the house. As she giggled and jumped and twirled, she suddenly noticed me in the distance. Her body came to an immediate stop as her attention riveted on me. For a few seconds she just stood there looking. I stood there looking back. Abruptly, she ran my direction, slowing as she approached the wire. She grabbed it with both hands and began swinging gently forward and back with her feet dragging and dancing on the ground, all the while her eyes focused on mine. Her gaze was studious, as if she was attempting to read me. I offered a gentle smile. She maintained her intense, examining countenance. She was still trying to sense her way forward.

Unexpectedly, she swung herself toward me and landed on both feet. Before stepping forward she glanced back at the two women laboring over the cauldron. One of the them gave an approving nod and smile. The little girl slowly walked over to where I was standing. Turning the direction I was facing, she stood beside me and mimicked my posture and hand positions. As I moved my hands to another position, she copied and giggled. There we stood watching the ladies wash clothes. She occasionally looked up sideways at my face. Each time I offered a smile. Each time she just looked.

Then something happened so pristine with loveliness it seemed like I was in another world. Suddenly, she reached her little hand up and clasped mine, looking up with a big smile. The ladies laughed.

When my friends came out of the house it was time to continue our journey. As we began to walk, my new little friend continued holding my hand and walked with us.

"I think it's time for you to go back to your mommy," I said gesturing with my free hand toward the ladies.

She was reluctant, and I was not eager, but her mother called her name in an emphatic tone. As best I could make out, her name sounded like Irene Enes. I was overwhelmed by her childish innocence and trust, and, of course, I felt frightened for her as well, fearing that someday her trust might be violated and her innocence stolen.

Only Children Enter

I am convinced that childlike innocence is the spirit that pervades heaven. In fact, I'm going to say something that may sound a little odd at first, but follow through with me:

God is a child at heart.

Responding to His very adult disciples as they tried to shoo away some children, the Savior said, "Let the little children come to Me, and do not forbid them; for of such is the Kingdom of God. Assuredly, I say to you, whoever does not receive the kingdom of God as a little child will by no means enter it" (Luke 18:16-17).

If nobody enters the kingdom of God except those who become like little children, it follows that the God who defines the spirit of that glorious place is Himself like a little child in some significant respects. As I know Him, God is a child in the basic makeup of His character. The Almighty Creator thinks and feels with motives of the purest innocence. He has never done wrong, has never violated a solitary creature, has never served Himself to the hurt of another being.

His heart is all laughter and joy at the wonders of existence, although currently He is in the throes of a painful struggle that you and I happen to be at the center of. "He was, is, and ever shall be divinely childlike. . . . Childhood belongs to the divine nature" (George MacDonald, *A Child in the Mist*).

God is not immature, but He is innocent.

He's not naive to evil, but evil is foreign to His nature.

He's not silly-minded, but He did design the penguin's waddle.

God is childlike in all the beautiful ways that a child is childlike, but on a mega-mature level.

No ego trip.

No affectation.

No manipulation or spin.

Just pure authenticity and unbridled love.

According to the prophets, who knew the divine heart by direct revelation, God is "of purer eyes than to behold evil, and cannot look on wickedness," and yet "the eyes of the LORD are in every place, keeping watch on the evil and the good," because while He can't bear to look, He can't refrain from caring (Habakkuk 1:13; Proverbs 15:3).

God weeps at our pain and collects all our tears in a bottle (John 11:35; Psalm 56:8).

God writes love songs and also rages with anger and agony at the things we do to hurt one another (Zephaniah 3:17; Isaiah 1; Genesis 6:5-8).

God took delight in having Adam name the animals in a game designed to prompt the man to realize he needed a woman, and God takes notice of every sparrow that falls dying to the ground (Genesis 2:18-23; Matthew 10:29).

Maybe God is younger than we think. Perhaps "we have sinned and grown old, and our Father is younger than we" (G.K. Chesterton).

No More Shame

The kingdom of this world and the prevailing ethos it generates, is basically a psycho-edifice built on a base of lies regarding the character of God, giving rise to walls of self-centeredness as the core human motive, which manifests in a greedy and insatiable appetite for more, and yet more, of whatever may be had to stimulate and then numb self, necessitating manipulation, deceit and control tactics (a.k.a. marketing), and covering its stench with just enough humanitarian efforts to justify our indulgence, gluttony, and lust (Romans 1:21-32; Ephesians 2:1-3).

The whole system is a shame-generating machine that pulls us into its jaws by means of the very shame it generates. That's what you call a *cycle*, and *this* cycle is lethal if allowed to run its course. Guilt is a deadly power that kills the soul one emotion at a time, driving our self-addicted appetites to smaller, and yet smaller capacity for other-centered love until there's nothing left of us but a gnawing sense of inward-focused desire that can't be satisfied (Ephesians 4:17-19).

But God has a plan for our healing.

Paul explains that the sacrifice of Christ was made in order to achieve what the symbolic sacrifices could not—to bring our hearts to a condition in which there is "no more consciousness of sins" (Hebrews 10:2). He then urges us to "keep our hearts pure, our consciences free from evil" (Hebrews 10:22, Bas). Jesus came to break the cycle of sin and guilt, to liquidate our shame by means of forgiveness and to restore eternal innocence to our souls. The Savior looked our shame straight in the eyes and denied it any existence as a barrier between Him and us. I don't "condemn you," He said, "go and sin no more" (John 8:11). Then He "endured the cross, despising the shame" (Hebrews 12:2). Crushed under the heel of all the enmity we could muster, He just kept right on loving us. "When He was reviled, [He] did not revile in return" (1 Peter 2:23). "Father, forgive them," He cried as we took His life. And in that single cosmic act of atoning love, our shame was repudiated. Now the innocence of eternal childhood could return to mankind.

Imagine a world in which all eyes easily meet without the slightest insecurity or discomfort.

A world in which it never occurs to anyone to be in competition with anyone else.

A world in which literally every person totally trusts every other person and it never enters their mind not to.

A world in which everybody feels completely affirmed and uninhibited.

A world in which nobody is guilty of anything, and everybody genuinely loves all others without reserve.

If you can envision that kind of world, you have some sense of what God is like and of the plan He has for you and me.

In its final form the universe at all levels will reflect God's heart as a perfectly harmonious social structure of self-giving love. Each citizen of that kingdom will love all others without any reserve, insecurity, or shame. A mature childlike innocence will reign eternal in every soul.

eighteen

U L T I M A C Y

ecently I woke up in the middle of the night crying. Not lightly, but a heavy weeping. In my dream, someone I love had died in a tragic accident. I was submerged under a profound sadness. It was so real and so intense. I lay there sobbing as I gradually awoke. Upon opening my eyes, a glad sense of relief gripped me as I realized it was just a bad dream.

There have been other times when I've had dreams so wonderful that I was disappointed to wake up and discover I was only dreaming, like the recurring one in which I dive into the ocean and a smiling dolphin takes me onto its back and we surge up and down through the water and then up out of the water through city streets.

What a ride!

And what a letdown to wake up dry!

Wouldn't it be incredible if all your good dreams came true and all your nightmares came untrue in the end?

What if all our desires for goodness, for beauty, and for love have been telling us the truth all along, harkening back to the way things were made to be in the beginning and reaching forward to the way things ultimately will be in the end? And what if all the living nightmares that haunt or world, all the evil and all the pain, were to sink into an eternal oblivion "as though they had never been"? (Obadiah 1:16).

Well, actually, this is precisely the vision and promise of the Bible. This hope is no fiction or figment of our imaginations. It is, in fact, an aspiration that is true to ultimate reality as God envisions it. We might even say that our desire for good to triumph and for evil to be banished from existence is a universal prophecy that continually retells in every human heart.

There is sufficient reason to believe that the core essence of every good dream will ultimately come true and that everything contrary to love will finally cease to be. Then we will be like the poet who said, "I dreamed I awoke to discover I had been dreaming all along, and the dream was true" (Unknown).

God Has Dreams Too

Scripture says that even for God our world's history is like a bad dream. When it's over, He will awaken and despise the horrific image of evil men doing their evil deeds:

"As a [bad] dream when one awakes, so, Lord, when You awake, You shall despise their image" (Psalm 73:20).

The One who created us for eternal relational bliss longs for the nightmare of evil to end, too, and He wants all our good dreams to become vivid, living realities. He has bright hopes and plans for our world and He is determined to see them through to fulfillment. Against all evil He stands arrayed in a severe love that cannot be stopped. With a steady march that has all the powers of darkness trembling, He will vanquish all horror and immortalize all goodness.

I remember so well the first time it dawned on me that God is angered and hurt by all the injustice and suffering in our world.

I was so relieved.

It was my eighteenth year of life. All I had known to that point was pain. Beyond my own little living nightmare, the nightly news had been talking a lot about the many children that were being abducted and sold on the underground slave market. It was more than I could bear to think of. In the immediate context of concrete evil, the idea that there might be an all-powerful God out there somewhere in the sky seemed ludicrous to me. My mom and my girlfriend were really getting into Jesus and studying the Bible. I thought, "Wow, how can they be so gullible and irrational. If there's a God worth knowing anything about, there is no way He would have created a world like ours. And a God who would make a world like ours would have to be a psychopath."

I wanted a Rambo or Terminator kind of God, I guess. I figured that if God did exist He'd simply lay waste to our world. Since He wasn't laying waste, I thought He most likely didn't exist. But if He did exist, I reasoned, well then, the world must be just the way He wants it to be, in which case I would be obligated to hate Him.

Then one day a whole new idea entered my mind: what if *love*, and not *control*, is God's ultimate objective for our world?

The prospect was tantalizing.

But the idea would have to make rational sense. There is no way I could have accepted the existence of God on the basis of religious authority or "blind faith," whatever that is. Since I was raised in a completely secular home with no religious education, the Bible meant nothing to me. It had no authority in my thinking. To me it was in the category of literature, on the same level with Shakespeare or the Greek myths. But suddenly, in the throes of my fury and frustration at all the horrible things going on in the world, this provocative new perspective started to take shape in my thinking, a perspective in which *love, freedom,* and *risk* were logically linked.

If love, rather than control, were God's ultimate goal for our world, a whole new framework of understanding would naturally follow. Something like this: To the possibility of love is the necessity of freedom, and to the necessity of freedom is the potential for both good and evil. Love, by its very nature, must be voluntary if it is to occur at all. A world in which wrongdoing would be impossible would be a world in which love would be impossible as well. So if love were the end-goal, freedom would be the only way to get there. Therefore, a world in which both good and evil are possible is the only kind of world in which good could eventually reign supreme and from which evil could be permanently eradicated.

Wow, the lights were really coming on.

Immediately, within this totally new perspective, it became plausible to my mind that a God of almighty power and perfect goodness could actually exist with a world like ours on His hands, and not be a monster. If love and not dominance was the ultimate value in play, a God of good character could exist and not Himself be culpable for the existence of evil. In fact, I began to realize that a God of love would Himself be the greatest sufferer of all in the face of evil. It became evident in this newly forming line of logic that a God who holds absolute power within the parameters of absolute love would choose to limit the exertion of His power in favor of preserving our freedom, so that by other means than sheer power can afford, good could ultimately triumph over evil. Methods of power, control, and coercion are simply antithetical to freedom and therefore incapable of generating love. The simplicity and explanatory power of this perspective was extremely enlightening and radically liberating. For the first time in my life I could grasp the logic of the existence of a good God.

In my seminars I have often illustrated the love-freedom-risk paradigm by asking those in attendance to imagine that I have a gun in my hand. I point the imaginary gun at the group and command, "Stand up!" Then I ask, "Would you stand up?" Everyone answers with a resounding, "Yes!" Then I ask, "If I were to point the gun at you and tell you to stand on your head, would you?" Again the answer is always, "Yes!"

Everyone agrees that behavior can be controlled by means of force.

But then I ask, "What if I were to point the gun at you and command, "Love me! Be my best friend! Trust me! Feel loyalty and affection for me!" Then I ask the revealing question: "Could you do it? Not, *would* you, but *could* you? Would it even be possible for you to experience such thoughts and feelings toward me while I relate to you with manipulation and coercion? In other words, can love be forced?" Everyone answers with a decided, "No!"

We know this intuitively, which is to say, we know it at the deepest level of our rational souls. And the reason we know it is because we were made in the image of a God whose essential character is non-coercive love. Our very natures recoil at the thought of force. Nobody has to teach us the truth of human freedom. We just know it. "We hold these truths to be self-evident, that all men are created equal, that they are endowed by their Creator with certain unalienable Rights, that among these are Life, Liberty and the pursuit of Happiness."

But if the simple but profound reality that love and freedom are inextricably connected is true, then aren't the implications equally true? When the Bible says, "God is love," isn't this just another way of saying that God is all about the voluntary exchange of trust, loyalty, faithfulness, and the like. And if God is love in this sense, then God is, by logical deduction, decidedly anti-coercion. And if God is anti-coercion, then it follows that He would have to genuinely give us freedom and allow us to do with it what we will, for better or for worse in each individual case. He must facilitate the conditions in which each one of us may utilize our freedom to whatever end we might choose, either to the eternal ruin that lurks within selfishness or to the eternal wellbeing that presides in self-giving love.

And so it came to pass that God's existence became a rational and even hope-filled belief in my mind,

and God's character became vindicated in my heart,

and God's love became the center of meaning in my view of reality as a whole,

and cooperating with God's plan for eradicating evil and immortalizing good became my life's passion.

I could now see that God's heart pulsates with desire for all human beings to be ushered into an ultimate reality of relational love, free from all violation and hurt. And soon I discovered that this picture of God, this love-freedom-risk theology, is completely exclusive to the God of the Hebrew Scriptures and to the person of Jesus Christ. The vision was so beautiful, and so intuitive to the human heart's desire for love and freedom, that I found it irresistible.

What other belief system showcases a God who thinks and feels and speaks like this:

"They shall not hurt nor destroy in all My holy mountain, for the earth shall be full of the knowledge of LORD" (Isaiah 11:9).

Here is the heart of our Creator.

Here is His dream for humanity.

Here is His most ardent desire and His most determined purpose for planet Earth and its inhabitants.

Can you imagine!

This is the God of the universe. So far from being the controlling, malicious dictator He's often made out to be, God actually has only one grand goal for our world: no more hurt and no more destruction.

If you find that your heart agrees with this ultimate objective, then eternity belongs to you.

If you find no resonance with the kind of world God dreams of, then you would never be happy in the eternity He has planned.

Life And Death

There's only one thing God is against, and that's anything that causes hurt and destruction. Sin alone falls into that category. Paul says:

"Love [agape] does no harm . . ."

Pause there before reading the remaining part of the verse.

Please notice that it is the nature of love to do no harm. This is the bottom-line reality with love. It is decidedly anti-violation and therefore anti-hurt. Love is the will, the motive, the passion to do only what is good and right toward all others.

Now let's finish Paul's statement:

"Love does no harm to a neighbor, therefore love is the fulfillment of the law" (Romans 13:10).

The law of God is here depicted as a law of love, as it is throughout all of Scripture.

The basic premise of this book is that human beings were originally engineered by the Creator for other-centered love rather than self-centeredness. We are not mere biological survival machines, but rather we are spiritual beings made for a high and beautiful relational bliss. We thrive in a moral climate of trust, loyalty, affection, and overall integrity. This is who and what we are by design. We are creatures made for a quality of love that does no harm.

By contrast, everything contrary to love causes harm and is therefore destined for oblivion.

"He who does not love his brother abides in death" (1 John 3:14).

According to the apostle John, death is directly linked to an absence of love. Love is the essential content of life as God made life to operate. Death occurs where love is missing. Current science of the last twenty years or so, as noted in chapter one, is proving this biblical truism. We know now as a matter of measurable scientific fact that human nature is designed to live and thrive within behavioral patterns of self-giving love, and that everything of an anti-love character is anti-life or pro-death at its core. By making this discovery, scientists are unwittingly vindicating the law of God as the concrete truth that undergirds all reality.

After making his declaration regarding death as an anti-love phenomenon, John goes on to give us perhaps the most succinct and comprehensive statement in the Bible regarding who God is and how He designed human life to function:

"God is love. Whoever lives in love lives in God, and God in him" (1 John 4:16, NIV).

God's love composes the structural content of life. Other-centeredness is the principle by which life is sustained in God's system. Love *is* life, and life *is* love, by definition. Life is a law-governed reality, and the law upon which it operates is love. God's love is the *rule* of life and therefore God's love *fuels* life.

Conversely, all anti-love thoughts, feelings, and behaviors inch the soul toward death. Death takes up space in the soul to the degree that we give ourselves over to self-serving pursuits. Death is composed of things like hatred, anger, greed, resentment, gossip, envy, lust, and dishonesty. This is why Paul says, "the wages of sin is death" (Romans 6:23). This is not intended to convey an arbitrary threat, but rather to describe the innate link between sin and death. To make himself absolutely clear, Paul later unfolds in more precise language the organic connection between sin and death by pointing out that sin is a "law," a principle of motive and action, that brings "death" (Romans 8:2). Then he states explicitly, "To be carnally minded *is* death . . ." (Romans 8:6). By contrast he says, "But to be spiritually minded *is* life and peace" (Romans 8:6). Then he articulates *why* death is integral to sin: "Because the carnal mind is enmity against God; for it is not subject to the law of God, nor indeed can be" (Romans 8:7). Again, Paul calls our attention to God's law as the code of life. Sin leads to death precisely because it is at enmity with God and His law. As Paul and all of Scripture explains, God's law is a reflection of His very character, which is self-giving love, and sin is "transgression of the law," or, in other words, rebellion against God's love. Sin is the perversion, or the inversion, of the soul from its divinely-designed outward orientation to a corrupted inward orientation. When Paul indicates that sin causes "harm" to others, he means that sin serves self to the injury of others. And when he says, "love is the fulfillment of the law," he means that those who live within the parameters of God's law live for God and all others before and above themselves. Therefore, sin is the law of death and love is the law of life.

Self As Center

In the Neverland dining room of the late Michael Jackson there hangs a triptych (a three-panel painting) commissioned by the singer with American artist David Nordahl. The right panel shows Jackson being knighted, a bodiless hand lighting a sword upon his shoulder. The left panel shows Jackson being crowned king, again by bodiless hands. The larger center panel is more striking still. It shows Jackson standing erect and muscular as a warrior clothed in medieval dress. He is wearing a brilliant gold and purple cape. His arms are lifted shoulder height with his hands resting on the handle of a large sword with its point on the ground before him. Part of the dark genius of the triptych is that it gives the impression that the bodiless hands that crown and knight Jackson are his own. He is utterly central to his own consciousness and totally self-sustained, which is emphasized by the six verses written over the sword to explicitly communicate the point of the paintings:

I am the thinker, the thinking, the thought.

I am the seeker, the seeking, the sought.

I am the dewdrop, the sunshine, the storm.

I am the phenomenon, the field, the form.

I am the desert, the ocean, the sky.

I am the Primeval Self in you and I.

Michael Jackson

Frighteningly isolating words!

If ever there were a dark psychological abyss, this is it. To see myself as subject and object, as cause and effect, as all there really is, could only become overwhelmingly limiting, isolating, and confining in the end. Such a self-view completely upends and inverts the meaning of life from an outgoing expansion of giving to an inward-focused collapsing in on oneself.

Jackson's poem captures well the only direction the human mind can see to go when God is erased from the picture or when God is defined as one's self. Either God or "Self" occupies the pinnacle of reality in each person's perception. Either love or self-love is the primary meaning of life in each person's basic motivational orientation. And the Bible tells us that there is life in the one frame of mind and death in the other.

Life Magazine asked Stephen Jay Gould, the now deceased Harvard scientist, "Why are we here?" He answered:

"We are here because one odd group of fishes had a peculiar fin anatomy that could transform into legs for terrestrial creatures; because comets struck the earth and wiped out dinosaurs, thereby giving mammals a chance not otherwise available. . . . We may yearn for a 'higher' answer—but none exists" (Quoted in Timothy Keller, *The Reason for God*, p. 36).

Gould failed to ask the more fundamental question present in his own answer: Why does this yearning for a "higher answer" exist in the first place? If there is no meaning to life beyond ourselves, as Gould suggests, then why do we "yearn" for a transcendent meaning?

Wouldn't it be strange if we are the way we are—longing for something grand and glorious to live for beyond ourselves—for no reason at all?

Filled with a yearning for an ultimate love that hails from nowhere and reaches out to nothing?

Pervaded by a nagging sense that someone is ultimately there for us, but no one really is?

Bertrand Russell, one of the most strident atheists ever to take up the cause, once wrote words that pulled back the veil from his own eyes for a moment of truth:

"Nothing can penetrate the loneliness of the human heart except the highest intensity of the sort of love the religious teachers have preached" (Bertrand Russell, *The Autobiography of Bertrand Russell*, p. 146).

Even Sigmund Freud, father of psychotherapy and hardcore atheist, toward the end of his life could not help but speak of "strange, secret longings . . . for a life of quite another kind" (Quoted in, Dr. Armand M. Nicholi, Jr., *The Question of God*, p. 243).

If we conclude that there is no ultimate "Other" to love and by which to be loved, then it is inescapable that we will conclude that there is no ultimate meaning to life beyond serving ourselves. The human heart loses its sense of value and meaning to the degree that self becomes the center of focus and motivation. As one's sense of self enlarges, one's sense of life's significance shrinks. The reason for this phenomenon is simply that the human heart only knows significance within the mental and emotional parameters of other-centered love. Such love is the essence of who God is, and human beings were made for life in fellowship with this God. And so, to live with self-centered focus constitutes a deep violation of one's own soul and of the true meaning of life, whereas to live within the awareness of God's love as the paramount reality of life will facilitate our return to our true humanity.

And what a noble dignity will be ours when we learn to be who we really are, when we become receptacles and dispensers of God's love!

Becoming Complete

In our journey together we have repeatedly called attention to the fact that every desire that surfaces in our hearts in favor of justice and against evil reveals that our humanity was originally designed in the divine likeness. Every yearning for love that stirs within our souls and every sense of repulsion at the horrors that pervade our world tell us we were made for something more. All our longings for goodness are longings for the One who is the source of all goodness.

Now we are at our journey's end, and what more is there to say but the same, from yet another angle.

So I will leave you with a song. In fact, it is the song of all songs, for that is its name, and rightfully so.

In an ingenious stroke of Spirit-inspired wisdom, King Solomon crafted a love story in song that curiously portrays the two lovers, himself and his lady, as bearing the same name.

Solomon is the masculine form of *shalom.*

Shulamite is the feminine form of *shalom.*

With poetic beauty and high spiritual significance, the song reveals Solomon courting the heart of Shulamite to the climactic place where her name finds union and resolve in his:

"Then I became in his eyes as one who found shalom" (Song of Songs 8:10, literal Hebrew translation).

Shalom *the woman* finds shalom *the experience* in Shalom *the man*. All she yearns for is experientially realized in the one who embodies those yearnings. She is at home in him, for he is the perfect companion to her deepest heart's desire.

We most commonly translate *shalom* as "peace." In Hebrew the word carries the idea of complete fulfillment, wholeness, a sense of total wellbeing in which nothing is missing. Shalom is the ultimate state of being, for it entails being exactly who and what you are suppose to be. In the song, Shulamite finds a sense of complete wholeness in Solomon's love. They are the perfect match. He *is* what she needs. Within his love she is totally fulfilled.

The story of the Bible is the story of another perfect match.

Between the human heart and the divine heart.

Between the One who is the source of all true love and those who desperately need His love for their eternal wellbeing.

That's where your story and mine has been tending all our lives.

Can you conceive of anything better than to be eternally loved with absolute goodness and faithfulness, and to experience that same quality of love forever flowing out of your heart to God and all others?

Of course you can't.

To know at the bedrock level of your soul that God is love, and that He loves *you*, is without question the most massively important and totally exciting discovery you'll ever make. The human imagination can reach no higher because there is, in fact, no higher reality to be conceived. God holds before us the best of everything we've ever dreamed of and more of the best forever escalating in our hearts to greater heights of fulfillment and forever cascading from our hearts to all others in an eternal stream of self-giving love.

It's not farfetched.

We can taste it even now,

in every moment of true friendship,

in every selfless act we perform or witness,

in every burst of innocent laughter,

in every feeling of trust and unreserved acceptance.

And if that's what this God named Desire offers, I'm in.

I hope you are too.